*Dedicated to
the Spirits of the Departed*

**'The Chewing Gum Girl'**
(see 'A Victorian Cemetery')

Photo: Mike Penney

# Death in Chester

**Roman Gravestones, Cathedral Burials, Martyrs, Witches, The Plague, Horrible Hangings, Gruesome Deaths and Ghostly Goings-on**

*TEXT BY*

## ROY WILDING ©2003

*DRAWINGS AND PUBLICATION BY*

## GORDON EMERY ©2003
## 27 Gladstone Road, Chester CH1 4BZ
01244 377955

*PRINTED BY*

The Bath Press

# CREDITS

Thanks to the staff of The Grosvenor Museum, Chester Archaeology, Chester Library, Cheshire and Chester Archives, and Chester Community Heritage Centre for their help. Thanks also to Len Morgan for his specialist knowledge of Overleigh Victorian Cemetery, Vincent Dunning and David A Ellis for the photo of the Gaumont Cinema, Simon Warburton for the picture of St John's Church, Mike Hewitt from Tourism, David Cummings for the engraving of the cow in Shipgate Street, Mike Penney for his photos, not forgetting the late Ray Mulligan (Blue Badge Guide).

## *Publisher's Note*

From the deaths of people in Chester over the last two thousand years we can see a little of their lives, their customs, their beliefs.

Roy has captured some of the more interesting features from Chester life and death as well as some of the most bizarre.

From graves and pictures to written records these deaths have given us an insight to the centuries.

But what of the poor souls who died sudden deaths - does some part of them or their vibration still live on in parts of the city? Here too are the unexplained phenomena.

# CONTENTS

*Death in Chester Amphitheatre*

# The Amphitheatre, Symbol of Death

### Blood, Sex and Gore

*"Once the Romans had arrived to create Deva (Chester), regular festivals
were all the rage, with scantily-clad maidens garlanding giant phalluses
(the ancient equivalent of maypoles) and everyone letting their hair
down to enjoy orgies.
Free large-scale public spectaculars including gladiatorial contests, chariot
races, and executions usually ended in debauchery.
Brothels and sophisticated bath houses proliferated.
Not surprisingly the ousted British tribes were soon avid to join in the fun,
and flocked eagerly to the port of Deva which,
soon populated by Greeks, Syrians, Germans, Africans and Gauls
became a throbbing cosmopolitan fleshpot.
Prostitution was legal, 177 days were specifically set aside
each year for festivals, and the idea that any of this alfresco eroticism
was sinful would have been laughable."*

Just to the southeast of the Newgate, above Souters Lane, is the most spectacular and dramatic survival of Roman Chester - the amphitheatre. A Roman legionary fortress would normally have an amphitheatre outside its walls, as would a large civilian settlement. These arenas were used not only for the sort of gladiatorial combats shown in epic films like *'Gladiator',* but also for military training exercises and public executions.

The stone-built amphitheatre structure appears to have replaced an earlier timber one. The oval area of the amphitheatre measured 59 metres by 50 metres, and it is thought that there was accommodation for more than 7,000 spectators. This, if judged in ratio to the size of the population then and now, would be equivalent to a modern stadium of at least 70,000 spectators. Amphitheatres were the product of incredibly skilful acts of political manipulation of the population: not only for the entertainment and pacification of the masses, but also to display the might and grandeur of the Roman Empire, particularly to hostile tribes.

## *Daughters of Darkness*

To the west of the north entrance of the amphitheatre is a strange little cell. This chamber served as a shrine of the Greek goddess Nemesis and contained a stone altar dedicated to her, which is now displayed in the Grosvenor Museum. The shrine was put up by a centurion Sextus Marcianus, *ex visu* (as a result of a vision). In Greek mythology, Nemesis was the goddess of retribution. She appears in the *'Theogony'* of Hesiod as the daughter of Nyx, the goddess of Night:

*Baneful Night bore Nemesis, too,
a woe for mortals*

Just prior to this mention of the birth of Nemesis, the poet Hesiod also makes reference to the dreadful power of some other daughters of Nyx, including the Fates and the Keres. Taken together, these daughters of Night were feared because of their ability to punish the transgressions of mortals.

***Altar to Nemesis from the amphitheatre.***

8

Considering Nemesis' position as the personification of retribution, it was thought best not to anger her: gladiators may have made offerings and prayers to her before entering the arena.

A slate relief of a *retarius,* a gladiator who specialised in fighting with a net, found in the very southeastern corner of the fortress and close to the amphitheatre is strong evidence that gladiatorial spectacles took place in the arena.

***Tile showing a retarius found in the southeastern corner of fortress Deva***

Army bases were places of imprisonment, so amphitheatres were used for retribution in the punishment and execution of prisoners. In the centre of the arena, archaeologists have found evidence of a group of irregular postholes set in shallow gullies, which was the base of a timber platform. This may either have been a permanent or temporary structure, erected and dismantled as required, and might have been a scaffold for public executions.

## *Heart-Throb*

*"The Roman appetite for excitement and violence seemed limitless".*

The first games, started in 238 BC, were no more bloodthirsty than a county fair. They featured exhibitions of trick riding, acrobatics, wirewalkers, trained animals, chariot racing and athletic events. There were boxing and wrestling matches, and the militia staged mock battles and drills. There was also horse racing and the occasional pageant. An admission fee was charged by whoever was producing the show.

Later, these sort of events got far too tame for the bloodthirsty Romans. The only one to last was the chariot racing, which was a perfect sport for gambling. However, even the chariot racing changed its character: it became bloody and more exciting to hold the interest of the masses. Like chariot racing, contests of gladiators probably originated as funeral games. However, these contests were much less ancient than the races.

The first recorded gladiatorial combat in Rome occurred when three pairs of gladiators fought to the death during the funeral of Junius Brutus in 264 BC, though others may have been held earlier. Gladiatorial games were called *munera,* since these were originally duties paid to dead ancestors. Among the Roman ruling classes there was an important social obligation to provide outstanding funeral rites for their dead.

There was an ancient Roman custom, dating back to prehistoric times, of having a few slaves fight to the death over the grave of some great leader. Originally, this ceremony had been a sort of human sacrifice and the souls of the dead slaves were supposed to serve the chieftain in the next world. The two sons of the dead Brutus decided to revive the tradition, not only to show how much they revered the memory of the father, but also to gain great status among their peers.

These events gradually lost their exclusive connection with the funerals of individuals and became an important part of the public spectacles staged by politicians and emperors, eager to gain popularity with the masses. The large numbers of wall paintings and mosaics depicting gladiators indicate the popularity of gladiatorial games. Graffiti often appeared on walls such as:

*"Thrax is the heart-throb of the girls."*

10

## The Greatest Show on Earth

*"A place without justice or mercy,*
*where only the smart or ruthless could survive."*

Gladitorial contests, like chariot racing, were originally held in large open spaces with temporary seating. As the games became more frequent and popular, there was need for a larger and more permanent structure. The Romans eventually designed a building specifically for this type of spectacle (called an *Amphitheatrum* because the seating extended all the way around the oval or elliptical performance area, which was covered with sand, *harena*). Like Roman theatres, amphitheatres were free-standing. Because they did not require natural hills, as Greek theatres did, they could be sited anywhere.

Early amphitheatres were built of wood, and Chester's is thought to have been a timber-framed construction built in the third quarter of the 70ADs, immediately after the establishment of the Roman fortress. However, stone amphitheatres proved to be much more durable. Towards the end of the first century, a stone building probably replaced the wooden one at Chester. It was abandoned by the middle of the second century. Shortly after 273AD, the arena was paved with sandstone flags and the amphitheatre enjoyed its longest continuous period of use. It was probably abandoned around 350AD. Its use after this date is unknown.

The spectator seating at the amphitheatre may have been protected from the elements by the use of retractable sailcloth supported by masts fixed into the outer masonry of the arena and cantilevered over the crowd. Also, there may have been an inner wall to the arena, made of heavy planks fastened to poles set into the floor. The natural instinct of a wild animal turned loose in a brightly-lit arena full of shouting people was to hug the wall of the structure. The purpose of the space between the outer and inner walls was to allow arena slaves to poke hot irons or burning straw through holes in the inner wall to drive the poor creatures into the centre of the arena.

Animal shows were an important part of the games. Dangerous animals such as lions, leopards, wild boars, bulls, starving mastiffs, bears (including polar bears) etc. formed an integral part of the horrific public spectacle of death, although many of the most exotic animals were sent to Rome.

## Mega-Stars

Gladiators (named after the Roman sword called the *gladius*) were mostly unfree individuals (condemned criminals, prisoners of war, slaves). Some gladiators were volunteers (mostly freedmen or very low classes of freeborn men), who chose to take on the status of a slave for the monetary rewards or fame and excitement. Anyone who became a gladiator was automatically *infamis*, beneath the law and by definition not a respectable citizen. A small number of upper-class men did compete in the arena (though this was explicitly prohibited by law), but they did not live with the other gladiators and constituted a special, esoteric form of entertainment (as did the extremely rare women who competed in the arena).

All gladiators swore a solemn oath (*sacramentum gladiatorium),* similar to that sworn by a legionary but much more dire:

> *"I will endure to be burned, to be bound, to be beaten,*
> *and to be killed by the sword "*
> *(uri, vinciri, verberari, ferroque necari).*

Paradoxically, this terrible oath gave a measure of volition and even honour to the gladiator.

Trained gladiators had the possibility of surviving and even thriving. Some gladiators did not fight more than two or three times a year and the best of them became popular heroes.

Skilled fighters might win a good deal of money and the wooden sword (*rudis)* that symbolised their freedom. Freed gladiators could continue to fight for money, but they often became trainers in the gladiatorial schools or free-lance bodyguards for the wealthy.

## Butchers

> *"Scissors cuts paper; Paper wraps stone; Stone breaks Scissors".*

There were many categories of gladiators, who were distinguished by the kind of armour they wore, the weapons they used, and their style of fighting. Most gladiators stayed in one category, and matches usually involved two different categories of gladiator. Modern scholars have identified several types of gladiator, including *Thracian, Secutor, Retiarius* and *Bestiarius.*

*Thracians* wore a wide-brimmed crested helmet with visor, high greaves on both legs, arm protector, very small shield, and short curved sword (similar to Spartacus).

*Secutors* wore an egg-shaped helmet with round eyeholes, greave on one leg, arm protector, legionary- style shield and sword (*scutum* and *gladius)*. The *secutor* was called a chaser probably because he was frequently paired with the *retiarius*, who used running as one of his tactics.

A *Retiarius,* a net-and-trident fighter, wore an arm protector, often topped with a high metal shoulder protector, large net, trident, small dagger, and no helmet. The *retiarius* was the only type of gladiator whose head and face were uncovered. Since he wore practically no defensive armour, the *retiarius* was more mobile than most gladiators but was also more vulnerable to serious wounds.

The *Bestiarius* was a special type of gladiator trained to handle and fight all sorts of animals. The *bestiarii* were the lowest ranking gladiators; they did not become as popular or individually well known as other types of gladiators. *Bestiarii* are mainly depicted without body armour, equipped with whips or spears, and wearing cloth or leather garments and leggings.

The manager of a gladiatorial troupe was called a *lanista*. He provided lengthy and demanding training in schools, called *ludi*, especially designed for this purpose and usually located near to the amphitheatre. The standard arrangement for a school was a rectangular building with an open court in the middle where the men could practice. Around the court ran a roofed passage with small rooms, or cells, opening into it rather like a cloister. Each man had his cell where he could be alone. There was a kitchen, a hospital, an armoury, quarters for the trainers and the guards, and even a graveyard. There was also a prison with leg irons, shackles, branding irons and whips. Opening into the prison was room used for solitary confinement with a ceiling so low a man couldn't sit up and so short he couldn't stretch out his legs.

## A Day at the Arena

The games began with an elaborate procession that included the combatants and was led by the sponsor of the games, the *editor*. In Rome during the imperial period, this usually was the emperor, and in the provinces it was a high-ranking magistrate. The parade and subsequent events were often accompanied by music played by instruments such as the water organ and the curved horn *(cornu)*.

The morning's events might begin with mock fights, possibly with displays of Roman military might, to impress the natives. These would be followed by displays, sometimes featuring trained animals that performed tricks, but more often staged as hunts *(venationes)* in which increasingly exotic animals were pitted against each other or hunted and killed by *bestiarii*.

The lunch break was devoted to executions of prisoners-of-war, criminals and Christians. The public nature of the execution made it degrading as well as agony and was introduced to serve as a deterrent to others. One form of execution in the arena was *damnatio ad bestias,* in which the condemned were cast into the arena with violent animals or made to participate indramatic reenactments of mythological tales in which the stars really died. Criminals were also forced to fight in the arena with no previous training. In such bouts death was a forgone conclusion, because the victor had to face further opponents until he was killed. Such combatants were not, of course, professional gladiators.

In the afternoon came the climax of the games: the individual gladiatorial combats, which were refereed by a *lanista*. These were usually matches between gladiators with different types of body armour and fighting styles. It is popularly believed that bouts began with the gladiators saying, "*Those who are about to die salute you*". However, evidence for the use of this phrase can only be found in a description of a *naumachia* staged by Claudius using condemned criminals, where the men supposedly said,

"*Ave, imperator; morituri te salutant* "(Suetonius, *Claudius* 21.6).

There were, however, many rituals in the arena. When a gladiator was wounded and wished to concede defeat, he would hold up his index finger.

At this point the crowd would indicate with gestures whether they wished the defeated gladiator to be killed or spared. Until recently, it was the popular belief that that thumbs down meant kill and thumbs up meant spare, but there is no recorded visual evidence of this. Written evidence states that *pollicem vertere,* to turn the thumb meant kill and *pollicem premere,* to press the thumb, meant spare. This, in fact, indicates that those who wanted the gladiator killed waved their thumbs in any direction, and those who wanted him spared held up closed fists. In any case, the sponsor of the games decided whether or not to give the defeated gladiator a reprieve, a *missio.*

Some authorities today think that the death signal was made by stabbing with the thumb at the spectators own chest meaning let him have it here and the signal for release was to extend the hand flat with the thumb bent under the palm. Others think that the thumb was only used to signal death, that if the man was to be reprieved the crowd waved their handkerchiefs (did Romans have handkerchiefs?). No one really knows, but perhaps crowds at different arenas had their own particular custom of signals.

If the gladiator was to be killed, he was expected to accept the final blow in a ritualised fashion, without crying out or flinching. Some scholars believe there was also a ritual for removing the bodies of dead gladiators, with a man dressed as Charon (ferryman of Hades) testing the body to make sure he was really dead and then a slave dragging the corpse with a hook through a gate called the Porta Libitinensis (Libitina was a death goddess).

## *The Final Curtain*

*"The growth, character, and final degeneration of the ludi
closely paralleled the growth, character and degeneration
of the Roman Empire. In the old, simple days of the Republic,
the games were simply athletic contests.
As Rome became a conquering power, the games became
bloody, ruthless and fierce, although still retaining the conception of fair
play and sportsmanship... When Rome finished her conquests
and became merely a despotic power, the games became pointlessly
cruel. Toward the end they were nothing but sadistic displays.
Shortly after this, the empire collapsed."*

Near the end, thousand of Gauls, Germans, Celts and Parthians were brought in to bolster the weakening might of Rome. These so-called barbarians had little or no interest in the games. One Parthian prince left the circus in disgust, remarking, *"It's no fun seeing people killed who haven't a chance."* As the emperors depended on these foreign auxiliaries for support, placating the Roman mob became less and less important.

In 325AD Constantine, the first Christian emperor, tried to put an end to the games but they still continued. However, in 365AD, Valentinian forbade sacrificing victims to wild beasts, and he made his edict stick. In 399AD the gladiatorial schools had to close for want of pupils.

In 404 AD, a monk named Telemachus leaped into the arena and implored the spectators to stop the fights. The angry mob promptly stoned him to death. However, the emperor Honorius was so furious at the killing of the monk, that he closed all the arenas and they were never reopened. In 549AD, after the fall of Rome, a Goth named Tolila held the last chariot race.

## *Dust in the Wind*

*"The world of the Roman games...*
*seems at first site to be unbelievable in its ferocity.*
*That couldn't happen now we hear ourselves saying.*
*But the Roman populace who screamed with laughter*
*at the sight of fellow humans, defenceless women and children,*
*as well as gladiators, being torn apart by beasts,*
*or roasted alive, or crucified, or hacked to death,*
*cannot be dismissed as safely ancient.*
*We only need to look into the mouths of the gas-chambers,*
*killing fields of Cambodia,*
*or the mass graves of Rwanda and Kosovo*
*to realise that the mob is always with us,*
*and it's always howling for blood."*

Today, it is almost impossible to realise that the highlight of a Roman soldier's week was once at Chester's now dry, sterile amphitheatre. Try standing in the middle of the arena and imagine a highly charged football match with thousands of supporters all around, chanting, jeering and screaming at you, and remember - the loser dies!

# Graham Webster Gallery of Roman Stones

*"Epigraphy the study of inscriptions:*
*One of the most important aspects of this period*
*(the Roman occupation of Britain)*
*is the sudden introduction of literacy*
*and the habit of the Romans to carve inscriptions*
*on stone and metal recording their names*
*and other actions of a public and private nature.*
*There are thus hundreds of commemorative stones, tombstones,*
*altars, proprietary marks...It is from this vast body of information*
*that we can piece together the history of the Province..."*
*(Graham Webster 'Roman Britain').*

## *Victorian Revelations*

In 1883 repairs were being carried out to a length of the city wall near to the tower known as Morgan's Mount, about halfway between the Northgate and the Water Tower. I. Matthews Jones, the City Surveyor, noticed that the interior of the lower courses of the wall contained fragments of Roman stonework, including part of a tombstone.

More extensive repairs to the walls took place in 1887, on a stretch between the Northgate and King Charles Tower. This time so many Roman stones were discovered that the work was extended, and even more were found. Like the stones recovered in 1883, they were all buried within the interior of the lower part of the wall. The sculptures and inscriptions on the stones made it clear that they had come from Roman cemeteries.

In addition to the inscribed stones there were also a number of sculptured panels. These had once decorated large tombs or funeral monuments. Since Roman law forbade the burial of the dead within a built-up area, the cemetery or cemeteries must have lain outside the fortress walls.

Overjoyed by these magnificent finds, the Chester Archaeological Society and other interested groups pooled their resources to examine the stretch of wall west of the Northgate. Between 1890 and 1892 more collections of inscriptions, tombstones and sculptures were recovered. Between 1883 and 1892, over 150 stones were found.

Although a few Roman stones had been found in Chester before this date and a number have been found since, the discoveries in the north wall in those nine years still remain one of the most spectacular archaeological finds in Britain. Many of these stones are now superbly displayed in the award-winning Graham Webster Gallery of the Grosvenor Museum.

There is no great mystery how and why these artifacts had been hidden for so long in the walls. Although law prohibited private individuals from disturbing graves in Roman times, it seems to have been common practice to use gravestones to reinforce defences:

> "Several towns in Gaul drew on their cemeteries when they set up defensive walls in the late third century, notably at Strasbourg and Neumagen; in Britain, Lincoln and London provide striking examples of this usage..." (R. P. Wright & I. A. Richmond 'The Roman Inscribed and Sculptured Stones in the Grosvenor Museum', Chester 1955)

However, even more spectacular finds may still be waiting to be uncovered. Only recently, fragments of a Roman funerary banquet tombstone were found inside a rock-cut grave at Heronbridge, on Eaton Road, Handbridge. The largest piece of the tombstone is now on display in the new foyer case at the Grosvenor Museum.

## A World of Colour

Today's stones don't do justice to the colour and excitement of the Roman world. A world of toil for soldiers was offset by the luxury and thrills of leisure time. Inside the fort strict army rule was enforced but outside were the temples, the amphitheatre, the traders, the whorehouses, and hundreds of brightly painted funeral stones depicting, on many, the richness of the deceased earthly life or the glory of an expected afterlife.

Amazingly, some of the sandstone used for the monuments did not come from the bedrock of Chester, but was hauled by wagon from better quality sandstone beds eight miles away.

## Into the Darkness

When Romans were at the point of death, their nearest relative present endeavoured to catch the last breath with their mouth. The ring was taken off the finger of the dying person. As soon as they were dead, the nearest relation closed the eyes and mouth of the dead body.

Then they called on the deceased by name, exclaiming, *have* or *vale*. The corpse was then washed, and anointed with oil and perfumes by slaves who belonged to the undertakers. A small coin was then placed in the mouth of the corpse, in order to pay the ferryman in Hades.

The corpse was laid out on a couch in the vestibule of the house, with its feet towards the door. It was dressed in the best robe that the deceased had worn when alive. Ordinary citizens were dressed in a white toga while magistrates wore their official robes.

If the deceased had received a crown for their bravery, it was now placed on their head. The couch on which they were laid was sometimes covered with leaves and flowers. A branch of cypress was also usually placed at the door of the house if the deceased was a person of consequence.

Funerals were usually called *exsequiae* or *funera justa*; the former term was generally applied to the funeral procession *(pompa funebris)*. There were two kinds of funerals, public and private: the public one was called *funus publicum*, where a herald invited the people to it. The private funeral was called *funus tacitum*, *translatitium*, or *plebeium*.

A person usually left a certain sum of money in their will to pay the expenses of the funeral; but if they did not do so, nor appoint any one to bury them, this duty devolved upon the persons to whom the deceased property was left. If they died without a will, then the responsibility for the funeral fell upon their relations according to their order of succession to the deceased's property. The expenses of the funeral were in such cases decided by an arbiter according to the property and rank of the deceased, whence arbitria is used to signify the funeral expenses.

When wealthy Romans died, funerals were conducted with great pomp and ceremony, which was, of course, not the case for persons in ordinary circumstances. In the early days of Rome, all funerals were performed at night. However, later on, rich people held elaborate funerals during daylight hours, so that they could show off their wealth. The poor were only buried at night, because they could not afford a funeral procession.

## Bring on the Clowns

The corpse was carried out of the house on the eighth day after death. A person called a *Designator* or *Dominus Funeris* regulated the order of the funeral procession, and was attended by *lictors* dressed in black. Heading the procession were musicians, who played mournful music. Next came mourning women, called *Praeficae,* who were hired to lament and sing the funeral song in praise of the deceased. Players and buffoons sometimes followed these. One, called *Archimimus*, represented the character of the deceased and imitated his words and actions. Then came the slaves whom the deceased had liberated, wearing the cap of liberty *(pileati)*; occasionally there were many, since the master sometimes liberated all his slaves, in his will, in order to add to the pomp of his funeral.

Before the corpse, people walked wearing waxen masks representing the ancestors of the deceased, and were clothed in the official dress of whom they represented; there were also carried before the corpse the crowns or military rewards which the deceased had gained.

The corpse was carried on a couch *(Lectica)*, to which the name of *Feretrum* or *Capulus* was given; but the bodies of poor citizens and slaves were carried on a common kind of bier or coffin, called a *Sandapila*. The Sandapila was carried by bearers, called *Vespae* or *Vespillones*, because they carried out the corpses in the evening. The couches on which the corpses of the rich were carried were sometimes made of ivory, and covered with gold and purple. They were often carried on the shoulders of the nearest relation of the deceased, and sometimes on those of freedmen.

The relations of the deceased walked behind the corpse in mourning; sons with their heads veiled, and daughters with their heads bare and their hair dishevelled, contrary to the usual practice of both. They often uttered loud lamentations, and the women beat their breasts and tore their checks, though law forbade this. The corpse was carried to the place of burning or burial, which according to law, was obliged to be outside the city.

## Drink and be Merry

After the dead person had been put to rest at the funeral, the friends returned home. They then underwent purification called *suffitio*, which consisted in being sprinkled with water and stepping over a fire. There were also other acts of purification called *exverrae* using a certain kind of broom. The mourning and solemnities with the dead lasted for nine days after the funeral. At the end a sacrifice was performed, called *Novendiale*.

A feast was given in honour of the dead, but it is uncertain on what day; it sometimes appears to have been given at the time of the funeral, sometimes on the Novendiale, and sometimes later. The name of the feast was *Silicernium*. After the funeral of great men, there was, in addition to the feast for friends of the deceased, a distribution of raw meat to the people, called *Visceratio*, and sometime a public banquet. Combats of gladiators and other games were also frequently exhibited in honour of the deceased. (See Chapter The Amphitheatre, Symbol of Death).

## Gone but not Forgotten

The Romans, like the Greeks, were accustomed to visit the tombs of their relatives at certain periods, and to offer them sacrifices and vaious gifts, which were called *Inferiae* and *Parentalia*. The Romans appear to regard the *Manes* or departed souls of their ancestors as gods; hence arose the practice of presenting to them oblations, which consisted of victims, wine, milk, garlands of flowers, and other things. The tombs were sometimes illuminated with lamps on these occasions.

In the latter end of the month of February there was a festival, called *Feralia*, in which the Romans were accustomed to carry food to the sepulchres for the use of the dead. The Romans, like ourselves, were accustomed to wear mourning for their deceased friends, which appears to have been black or dark-blue, under the Republic, for both sexes. Under the Empire the men continued to wear black in mourning, but the women wore white. They laid aside all kinds of ornaments, and did not cut either their hair or beard. Men appear to have usually worn their mourning for only a few days, but women for a year when they lost a husband or parent.

# Beyond the Veil

The Sepulchral Banquet type of relief was first found in pre-Roman, Assyrian, Etruscan, Greek monuments, and around forts on the Rhine frontier. The reclined figure of the departed is celebrating their own life and death, and the passing of the soul to the Blessed Isles. It is as if the deceased (represented on the stone) is present with the mourners at their own wake, proposing a toast in a *poculum* or cup. The tripod table (or three-legged stool) is full of rich offerings. No evidence of the significance, if any, of the three-legged stool's constant presence on Sepulchral Banquet stones can be found. It may just be due to its everyday use in Roman life. However, three supporting legs do sometimes represent stability.

Described below are the majority of stones on display in the Graham Webster Gallery at the Grosvenor Museum, Chester. The Museum's system of numbering has been retained and given below, while the number in brackets come from the main reference source R. P. Wright & I. A. Richmond *The Roman Inscribed and Sculptured Stones in the Grosvenor Museum, Chester* 1955. This uses the same numbering system as the Catalogue of 1900.

### Stone No. 21 (108)

*To the memory of the departed, Curatia Dinysia aged 40 years; erected by her heir.*

This stone shows the dead lady enjoying a banquet. She reclines on a couch. In her hand Curatia holds a drinking cup. A three-legged tripod stands in front of the couch. Above the stone are two birds perched on garlands of leaves. Birds were thought to bring good fortune and to represent the souls freedom to escape after death. At the top corners are tritons, half-men, half-fish, blowing on seashell horns. This connection with the sea reflects the belief that the souls of the dead travelled across the ocean to a happier life in the Isles of the Blessed.

## Stone No. 20 (115)

*To the departed spirits of Flavius
Callimorphus, aged 42, and Serapion,
aged 3 years and 6 months. Thesaeus set
this up to brother and son.*

On this tombstone a gabled niche contains
a funeral couch with baluster legs,
mattress, cushion and high ends, upon
which reclines Callimorphus with Serapion
held close. The legs of the couch rest
upon high blocks, between which stands
to the right a three-legged dining table, on
which perches a tiny bird, and to the left a
carrot-shaped wine-jar. It was found in 1874 with two skeletons, a gold
ring, and a 'second bronze' coin of Domitian, in making a sewer along the
West Walls, about 12 metres from the walls and not far from the junction
with Grosvenor Road, that is southwest of the Roman fortress.

It is not clear whether the boy was the son of Callimorphus or Thesaeus.
The monument probably dates from the end of the first century or the
beginning of the second century A.D. The names Callimorphus, Thesaeus,
and Serapion are Greek. They may have been freedmen or traders.

## Stone No. 16 (65)

*To the spirits of the departed and
Aurelius Lucius, cavalryman. His heir
had this made.*

The exotic scene on this stone shows
the bearded man Aurelius reclining on
a couch. He holds up a drinking cup in
his right hand. His short sword and
helmet, complete with plume of
feathers are displayed. In front are a
three-legged table, a boy attendant or
slave and a single severed head. The
man holds his scrolled will in his left
hand.

The Romans usually recruited their cavalry from the less civilised parts of the Empire. Aurelius' appearance with a large fearsome moustache and stiff spiky hair suggests that he came from a barbarian background. This impression is increased by the severed head, which may represent a trophy from head hunting during a battle or raid.

The lower section is roughly marked as if intended to be put into the ground.

### Stone No. 22 (113)

*To the spirits of the departed, ... ] mina (bottom part of stone is missing and only part of the inscription remains).*

In this example a large seashell canopy has a dolphin either side. The lady who has died reclines on her couch. She holds a cup in her right hand. On the other a ring adorns her little finger. Beneath the couch is the usual three-legged table.

The seashell and the dolphins are a reference to the voyage of the lady's soul across the sea to the Isles of the Blessed.

## The Cavalry

*"The Roman Imperial Army was one of the most formidable fighting machines the world has ever seen; superb in its equipment, training and discipline, it was imbued with the deep Roman sense of the fulfilment of destiny in accordance with the designs of the gods. It was composed of the legions, heavily armoured infantry, all Roman citizens and some 5,000 strong, and auxiliary units, 500 strong (from the second century AD some were 1,000) trained and equipped as cavalry, infantry and mixed units.*

*There were also fleets for coastal and river patrols and transporting men and supplies. All this required a vast supporting organisation for supplies, armaments, communications, transport, recruitment and training etc. The legions were the main fighting force of the first and second centuries and also became the*

*builders and engineers responsible for the forts (like Chester)
and frontier works like Hadrian's Wall.*

*The army was in a constant state of change to meet the new enemies
and pressures from without. In the third and fourth centuries
it became far more mobile with points of static defences held by the old
traditional units, but the brunt of the fighting was borne by
the new field armies, almost entirely mounted and heavily armoured"*
Graham Webster *'Roman Britain'.*

### Stone No. 15 (99)

*To the spirits of the departed,
(rest of the inscription is missing).*

A fragment which, when it was
complete, commemorated a
Roman cavalryman. However, it is
also a propaganda message to all
would-be enemies of Rome. It is
symbolic of the ascendancy of
mighty Rome over all its
adversaries. A wounded barbarian,
the noble savage, his naked body
beautifully modelled, lies under the
legs of the cavalryman's horse, his spear broken and he clings to his
six-sided shield. Both his sword-belt and the hilt of his sword can be seen.

### Stone No. 18 (137)

*Inscription missing*

The rider is a Sarmatian, a nomadic
people who once lived north of the
River Danube in an area now known
as Hungary and western Romania.
The Sarmatians were defeated in
175AD by the Roman Emperor
Marcus Aurelius. The Romans then
forced them to contribute Sarmatian
men to their army.

25

Some were posted to Britain, including a force that was stationed at Ribchester in Lancashire. It may be that the rider on this stone was on detachment from Ribchester when he died at Chester.

The cloaked horseman holds aloft with both hands a dragon-ensign or pennon of Sarmation type, while his tall conical cap (as shown on Trajan's column), with vertical metal frame, is of Sarmation pattern. A sword hangs at his right side, and he is probably clad in scale armour. This attire for man and beast is characteristic of Sarmation cavalry. One authority suggests that the relief might depict a cavalryman taking part in the *Ludus Troiae* and dressed in eastern fashion.

The dragon-standard, for which the Sarmations were known and feared, consisted of a bronze dragon's head with fanged jaws wide open, mounted on top of a large pole. The back of the dragon's head was also open, and onto it was fastened a long tube made out of brightly coloured fabric. The size and shape of the holes in the dragons head were cleverly made. When the horseman rode into battle at full gallop, the wind rushed into the dragon's mouth. The force of the wind not only filled the tail out (like a windsock) but also made a terrifying sound like a shrieking 'banshee'.

### Stone No. 7 (91)

*Sextus Simil[...], son of Sextus, of the Fabian voting-tribe, from Brixia (now Brescia, in North Italy),.*

The dead man Sextus is shown mounted on his walking horse with a boy attendant or slave, who is leading carrying an oval shield and two javelins. The rider sits on a small saddle with prominent back and front, resting on a large saddlecloth. His horse has a well-groomed mane. The attitude and proportions are reminiscent of Greek models. The attendant, in Greek fashion, wears a pointed hat, but other features are somewhat defaced.

At the top of the stone is a bust of Sextus.flanked by two lion's heads, open-mouthed with tongues protruding, and with the heads of rams in their paws. Lions are often shown on Roman tombs. They are the symbols of the suddenness of death.

There were two kinds of horseman in Chester. One belonged to the cavalry wing, made up of auxiliary soldiers recruited in the less prosperous and civilised parts of the Empire. In addition there was a small number of horsemen attached to each legion to act as scouts and messengers.

## *Standing Figures*

### **Stone No. 30 (120)**

*Inscription missing*

This relief was once mistaken for a bishop and female acolyte, and became notorious as the ecclesiastical stone. It is, of course, of Roman origin. On the left stands an elegant lady clad in a full length tunic with long pointed sleeves, a stole or scarf covering her shoulders, with straight fringed hanging ends, and a jabot (ornamental fringe). In her left hand she holds a mirror, with a knobbed handle. Her head, now defaced, had a richly braided coiffure.

At her left side stands a little maidservant or slave, with long-sleeved tunic and folded arms, on which rest a toilet-box or tray, with indistinguishable objects upon it. Her little face, with small full mouth, is now mutilated.

## Stone No. 3 (38)

*To the spirits of the departed, Caecilius Avitus, of Emerita (Emerita was a colonia in Lusitania, now Merida in Spain), optio of the Twentieth Legion, Valeria Victrix, served 15 and lived 34 years. His heir had this erected.*

This complete stone shows a bearded *optio*, Caecilius Avitus. He was a junior officer, second in rank to a Centurion. His duties included some bookkeeping for the century, so he holds his accounts. He is dressed in a heavy cloak called a *sagum*, of which the ends cross and hang down his front in two tails. his right hand holds a tall staff. A sword, with massive round pommel, hangs on his right side. Below the cloak a kilt reaches to his knees. The lower parts of his legs are thick and stumpy.

## Stone No. 9 (37)

*To the spirits of the departed, Manius Aurelius Nepos, centurion of the Twentieth Legion, Valeria Victrix, lived 50 years; his most dutiful wife had this set up.*

The letter before AVR in the second line resembles the usual symbol for Manius, not Marcus. However, Manius is rare and aristocratic *praenomen*; while Marcus Aurelius is common in all cases. So it may be supposed the mason's chisel slipped.

This tombstone is made of cream-coloured Manley sandstone. A flat top niche holds the figures of the centurion Marcus Aurelius Nepo and his wife. Nepos is bare-headed and has a clipped beard. He holds a centurion's straight staff in his right hand. No attempt has been made to distinguish his tunic or corselet, but a cloak, draped over both shoulders, is fastened on his right shoulder by a knee-fibula, while a very wide belt is fastened low by a circular clasp above a full kilt falling to the knees. His legs and, in particular, arms are attenuated.

His wife, who erected the tombstone and whose name was never added, figured on a smaller scale stands higher in the niche, on a step level with Nepos' knees, as if in the background. Minute legs peep from below a full skirt, over which falls a draped over-skirt, which she holds up with her left hand. A distaff appears to be tucked into the waist under her left arm. Her right hand carries an indistinct object, perhaps intended for a weaving comb. Her hair is arranged in tight waves, of early third-century fashion.

In a recessed panel on the left side of the stone, beneath a stonemason's set-square and hammer is the formula: *dedicated while still under the hammer*. This formula was used extensively in Illyria, Cisalpine Gaul and in Transalpine Gaul, particularly in the Rhone valley; this is the only instance yet found (up to 1955) in Britain. It seems to mark a rite of dedication to make the tomb inviolable and place it under divine protection.

### Stone No. 11 (90)

*To the Spirits of the departed, Aerelius Diogenes, Bearer of the Imperial Effigy.*

The tombstone of an *Imaginifer*, one of the many types of standard bearer in the legion. The standard that he carried was a bust of the reigning Emperor or a member of the Imperial family. It would have been made out of silvered or gilded sheet metal. The long wooden pole with handgrips can be seen: the standard tied with a scarf-like *vitta*.

Diogenes is a Greek name, implying that he may have been from, or had some connection with, the eastern half of the Empire. He wears a military tunic and a cloak (sagus) which falls in two points in the front.

# Age of Mythology

*"The Roman government was very tolerant towards natives' religions,
unless, like Judaism and Druidism, they had a nationalistic aspect.
As newcomers, the soldiers, traders and civil servants
wished to make peace with the local gods and so
accepted, added and even identified many of them with
the classical deities. Thus one has altars which record vows
calling on the gods for aid in personal enterprise, often bearing two or
more names. The Roman god Mars was thus equated with the Celtic
Cocidius, Minerva with the healing god Sul at Bath.*

*All natural things like rivers, springs and hills had their own gods
and there were spirits that looked after every human activity
in addition to the greater gods of battle, trade and crafts, health and so on.
There were many shrines and temples were one could seek help and
advice from the particular god or spirit
and nothing was done without this essential step.*

*Religion, which gave deep personal feelings or sense of brotherhood,
came from the East and principal among them were
Mithraism and Christianity, which were great rivals in the third century AD.
The former consisted of small groups of soldiers and traders banded
together for protection and mutual assistance
(somewhat akin to modern freemasonry).
They worshipped in underground vaulted chambers
resembling the cave in which Mithras was born. The rituals were highly
secret and little is known about them, but there were seven grades of
initiates who underwent trials and ordeals to prove their faith.*

*Christianity became supreme because it included women
and had an organisation which appealed to the Emperor Constantine,
but he hedged his bets by still allying himself to the invincible Sun god,
on all his coins and inscriptions. The idea of the host of invisible spirits
helping or hindering us has survived even today as superstition "*
*(Graham Webster 'Roman Britain').*

## Not on display (169)

*No inscription*

In 1853, a complete stone was found built into the wall of a cellar in White Friars; it shows a cross-legged youth, dressed in cloak, tunic and Phrygian cap (Phrygia was an area in modern Turkey). In his right hand he holds a reversed torch. This is *Cautopates*, one of the two attendant deities of Mithras, and his occurrence implies the existence, at Chester, of a *Mithraeum*.

## Stone No. 27 (171)

*No inscription*

The headless figure of a crossed-legged youth with hands spread out as if in worship. He was probably the companion of one of the Eastern gods, such as Mithras or Attis. The attitude of the figure would fit *Cautes*, the fellow deity of *Cautopates*, but lack of detail precludes certainty. The stone was found in 1891 in the north wall, and was originally freestanding.

However, the two figures on the stones do not match, which may imply, if the first figure is Cautopates and the second Cautes, more that one *Mithraeum* at Chester.

31

## Stone No. 25 (170)

*No inscription.*

A standing figure of the youthful god Attis, He was the consort of Cybele, the mother goddess, whose worship spread from the Middle East throughout the Roman Empire. The cult had mysterious rites that promised life after death. Atti's death was mourned for two days in the Spring, and his recovery (when his spirit passed into a pine-tree and violets sprang up from his blood) then celebrated. Most Romans shied away from the extreme rituals such as self-castration.

On this stone he wears a tunic, cloak and Phrygian cap. He is shown as a shepherd carrying a crook. The figure faces slightly towards the left, as if one member of an opposed pair, flanking a tomb.

## Stone No. 29 (168)

*No inscription*

A coping stone from the surround of a funeral monument found, in 1848, in Handbridge, among sepulchral remains near the Roman road. A freestanding lion, the symbol of all devouring death, crouching over its prey, apparently a stag.

### Stone No. 26 (140)

*No inscription*

A sculpture showing a nude curly headed youth with a cloak over his right shoulder. He lies dying in the shade of a Carob tree, the type of tree indicating that the scene is set somewhere in the Middle East. The stone probably represents the death of Adonis, who was the favourite of the Roman goddess Venus, also identified with the Greek goddess, Aphrodite, goddess of love (her cult was of Eastern origin, and she was identified with Astarte, Ishtar etc).

The legend goes that Adonis was killed by a boar, but was restored to life by Persephone; Zeus decreed that Adonis would spend part of each year with her and the rest on earth with Aphrodite The use of the myth reflects the hope that the deceased will enjoy a new life beyond the grave.

### Stone No. 24 (141)

*No Inscription*

A relief of a Harpy, a mythical women-headed bird, which was figurative of death or its messenger. According to a legend told by Homer, Zeus blinded an evil king because of the king's cruelty. Zeus then gave orders that whenever a meal was placed before the king, the Harpies should swoop down and foul the food so that it was unfit for the king to eat.

## Stone No. 31 (172)

*No inscription*

A statuette of a goddess or genius (guardian spirit) seated in a stone recess. She wears a crown, holds a dish in her right hand and a large cornucopia (horn-of-plenty) in her left. The statuette may have come from a shrine.

## Stone No. 33 (138)

*No inscription*

**Left:** Hesione, naked and bound, stands on a rock to the left. Her head is defaced. Hercules (Greek and Roman hero of prodigious strength, who performed twelve immense tasks or labours imposed on him by Eurystheus, and after death was ranked among the gods), bearded and wearing only a cloak over his left fore-arm, brandishes his club in his right hand. He advances to attack the monster, which occupied the missing right third of the scene. The subject is an allegory of salvation.

**Right:** An anguipes or serpent-footed monster, figurative of evil. This is not, as was once suggested, the monster attacking Hesione, but a figure from a different scene on the adjoining face of the tomb.

## Stone No. 34 (139)

*No inscription*

In Greek mythology, Actaeon was a hunter who, because he surprised the goddess Artemis (Diana) bathing naked with her nymphs, was changed into a stag and ripped to death by his own hounds.(Another story claims it was because Acteon boasted of his superiority in the chase) Artemis was the virgin goddess of chastity and hunting; daughter of Leto; twin sister of Apollo.

On this stone, the nude Actaeon tries in vain to ward off the savaging hound on his left and the damaged stone preserves a suggestion of another hound attacking from his right. He is already part stag, for his bearded head sprouts antlers.

## *Grosvenor Museum and Shop*

27 Grosvenor Street ℂ 01244 402008   *Free admission*
*10.30 - 5.00 Mon - Sat, 2.00 - 5.00 Sun*

For further information on Roman Chester, or any other areas of history or archaeology, a visit to the museum is well worth while. As well as the superb Roman stone collection there are other Roman artifacts, temporary exhibitions, Stuart, Georgian and Victorian rooms and a staff willing to answer questions. In the shop an excellent range of books and fact sheets are available.

# The Jewel of St John's

## The Legend of the White Hind

St John's Church is magnificent and mysterious; steeped in power, myth and legend. Standing in a dominant position, on a red sandstone bluff above an ancient quarry, on the banks of the River Dee. On the same bluff, just to the west of the Church, is the ancient Roman Amphitheatre. The origins of this sacred place are lost in the mists of time. One Tradition goes that King Aethelred of Mercia founded St John's, in AD 689, after his Vision of the White Hind, which represented a symbol of purity :

*When Foregate Street was a track through the forest which was then outside the ancient walls of Chester, King Aethelred minding to build a church, was told that he should see a white hind, there he should build a church, which hind he saw in the place where St John's now standeth.*

Another account states that:

*This Saxon Church was erected about the year AD 906, by Ethelred, Earl of Mercia, and Ethelfleda his wife, the daughter of Alfred the Great; this view is strengthened by the finding of some Saxon Coins on March 4th 1862.*

In fact, both stories may have some basis of truth because, for generations, churches have been continuously built on the same site. A good example is Chester Cathedral, where it has been suggested that, under the Romans, the site was occupied by the Church of St Peter and St Paul, which, under the Anglo-Saxons, became the Church of St Werburgh. However, absolute evidence of such practice comes from further afield in London: where the church of All Hallows was built on the Roman Temple of Mithras. Although there is no archaeological evidence, it is not unreasonable to suggest that, perhaps, even a pagan temple stood on the St John's site in Roman times, associated with the Amphitheatre.

It is known for sure that Peter, Bishop of Lichfield (1072-85), transferred his see to Chester in 1075 and that his successor, Robert de Limesey (1086-1117), removed it to Coventry in 1102. During the intervening 27 years St John's Church was the cathedral of the diocese, and it is said to have retained the status of a cathedral even after the removal of the see to Coventry.

## The Collapse of the Tower

A dramatic event that occurred on the evening of the 14th April 1881 changed drastically the landscape of Chester forever. The Rev Samuel Cooper Scott, then vicar of St John's describes the event graphically:

> *I was aroused by a rumbling noise, which was succeeded by a*
> *terrible and indescribably long drawn-out crash, or rather rattle,*
> *as though a troop of horse artillery was galloping over an iron road;*
> *this was mingled with a clash of bells,*
> *and when it had increased to a horrible and almost unbearable degree,*
> *it suddenly ceased, and was succeeded by perfect stillness.*

*The collapse of St John's tower*

Happily, no one was injured or killed but, in its collapse, the tower demolished the church's Early English porch, which was never replaced due to lack of money.

## The Masons' Marks

From outside, the church looks Victorian, due to heavy restoration by R C Hussey between 1860 and 1866. Inside, the nave and crossing of the church is pure Norman work of the early 12th century. Of particular interest and rarity is the large number of early Norman masons' marks.

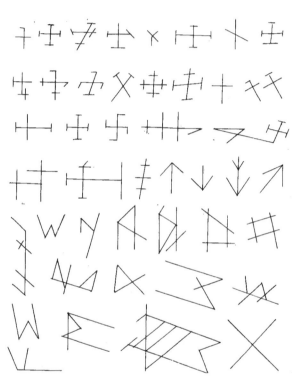

One mark that frequently occurs is what is now commonly known as the Swastika, a symbol adopted by the Nazis. The Swastika is a primitive and ancient symbol or talisman in the form of a cross with equal arms, each arm having a limb of the same length projecting from its end at right angles, all in the same direction (usually in the direction of the sun's course, i.e. clockwise).

The symbol is found in various parts of the world, especially Mexico, Peru, and Tibet. The name Swastika is from the Sanskrit svastika or svasti, meaning well being, good fortune or luck. It is strange, but not uncommon, to find pagan symbols in a Christian church, a reminder of past pagan beliefs and superstitions.

**Masons' marks at St John's Church**

The purpose of the other marks may include the individual mason's mark, to identify his work for quality checks or payment; structural location marks to indicate the location of the masonry in the course of building; or quarry marks for location and transportation of the stones to the building site. Some marks may just be graffiti.

38

## Celtic Crosses & Rare Gravestones

In 1870, the Duke of Westminster directed that the accumulations of earth, which concealed much of the ruins of the choir and its chapels, should be removed; in this process were discovered some wonderful crosses which are now displayed at the rear of the Nave.

**Crosses at
St John's Church**

Originally, they were considered to be of Welsh origin, but are now thought to be from workshops, reputedly established in the quarry of St John's by Irish - Norse traders who settled in Chester during the 10th century. Similar crosses from the same workshop have been found in many places over the Wirrall, on Hilbre Island and at Whitford in North Wales.

Displayed alongside the Celtic crosses in the nave are four 14th century gravestones. Three of the stone slabs graphically indicate the occupations of the deceased: An effigy of a priest; a Master Smith of the 14th century - blacksmith's horseshoe, hammer & tongs; a Master Glover -  scissors, wand & glove (leather work was the prime industry of Chester). The fourth stone shows an effigy of a lady with vine leaves:

*Here lies Agnes, wife of Richard de Ridleigh*
*who died on the Sabbath next before the*
*feast of Phillip and James the Apostle 1347.*

*Stone for a*
*Master Glover*

*Effigy of Agnes,*
*wife of*
*Richard de Ridleigh*

## The Anchorite Cell

Standing between St John's Church and the River Dee, below the church in the old quarry, is the 'Anchorite's Cell' (anchorite: hermit or recluse). This is a medieval hermitage, which was restored during the 19th century. It is a red sandstone building of two floors. Tradition asserts that King Harold II, after the battle of Hastings in 1066, came to Chester and ended his days in a cell here as a hermit.

## The King is Dead, Long Live the King

King William I was born in Falaise, France, the illegitimate son of Robert, Duke of Normandy. Robert, a descendant of the Vikings, was very cruel, and was known as Robert the Devil. In 1051, William visited his cousin, King Edward the Confessor. According to William, Edward, who was childless, named him as his heir.

In 1064, Harold Godwinson, Earl of Wessex, was shipwrecked on the

Normandy coast. William took him prisoner, and made him swear to uphold his claim as the price of his freedom. In January 1066, King Edward died and, on his deathbed, named Harold as his successor ignoring Harold's earlier promise to William, and so Harold was crowned as Harold II. Harold's brother, Earl Tostig, allied himself with Harold Hardrada (hard-ruler) King of Norway, and with William to seize the throne.

Harold Hardrada invaded England on the 25th September 1066, but Harold II defeated both Hardrada and Tostig in battle at Stamford Bridge, in Yorkshire. However, on the 28th September 1066, William and his army invaded England and landed near Pevensey, Sussex. Harold raced back from Yorkshire and, as everyone knows, his army was defeated at Senlac (Bloody) Hill, near Hastings on the 14th October 1066. History also records that Harold was killed at this battle, possible by an arrow in the eye.

*'Here, King Harold is dead' - from the Bayeux Tapestry*

When the Battle of Hastings was finally over, the unrecognisable body of King Harold lay in a pool of blood, the shaft of an arrow protruding from his left eye. His once fearsome Housecarl bodyguards were slaughtered around him like great broken axes. His body was so badly mutilated that William sent for King Harold's mistress, the so-called Edith Swan Neck, to identify him.

In the Life of Harold (Vita Harold) written by a monk at Waltham Abbey, it is stated that Harold was not killed but did, in fact, escape to Denmark to seek refuge with his cousin King Sweyn. Later in his old age (he would have been 51 years old at the battle), he returned to England. He spent a decade as a hermit in a cave in the cliffs of Dover. Later, he travelled north and west, settling for a time in the Welsh border country in Shropshire:

*his face hidden with a cloth so that he had to be guided as a blind man.*

41

Growing old, he made Chester his final home.

Giralde Cambrensis, in his book, states that Harold had many wounds and lost his left eye *with a strook of an arwe (a stoke of an arrow), and was overcome, and escaped to the country of Chester, and lived there holily an ankers life in Seint Iames celle faste by Seint Iohn chirche, and made a gracious ende, and that was I knowe, by his laste confession.*

History does state that Harold's wife, Algitha, took refuge after the battle in the Anglo-Saxon stronghold of Chester, and so this city would seem an obvious choice of refuge for a defeated prince of the Saxons.

In 1069, William went on to conquer the north of England; burning villages and crops, causing famine, rape and murder. In 1087, William was fatally injured when defending his Normandy territories. On his deathbed he sought forgiveness for the terrible destruction he had brought about in England. He died and was buried at Caen; his body was so fat and big for its coffin that two soldiers had to jump on it to force it in, and his intestines exploded in the process.

The survival of Harold after the battle of Hastings is an incredible story, but the next story depends upon a belief in the supernatural!

## *The Return of the King*

From time-out-of-mind, the legend of the ghost of the Saxon monk of St John's has been part of the folk-culture of Chester. The church and surrounding area is supposed to be haunted by the ghost of a tall hooded monk, which has been sighted many times over the generations. In 1941, a man and a young Franciscan friar were walking in the grounds of St John's when:

*The apparition, dressed in monk's habit with hood up, approached the two men. He was a frightening sight, so it was little wonder they moved quickly away but with amazing speed the apparition confronted them again. The unusual aspect of this encounter was that the ghost spoke to them in a guttural German accent. Both (men) had a keen interest in languages and later discovered it to be Anglo-Saxon, a very old language spoken in England between the 7th and 10th (11th and later) century.*

About midnight on a cold clear night just before Christmas 1973, a man was making his way to his home in Handbridge, by using the cobbled footpath that runs down to the river on the west-side of St John's and the old Hermitage, as

***The cobbled alley beside St John's Church***
*Photo: Mike Penney*

a short-cut, when:

*Suddenly to his amazement, a man dressed in a monk's black robe, cowl and sandals confronted him. The monk spoke to him in what seemed like German...When he told the monk that he could not understand him, the strange figure seemed very distressed and extended his hands as if pleading to be understood. The man repeated that he was very sorry but he could not understand him, and stepped aside and continued on his way home. The man, however, feeling sorry for the poor stranger, turned around hoping that he might still be able to help the monk in some way but, much to his astonishment, the monk had vanished! Now the little cobbled pathway is bounded on both sides by two high walls and there are no openings that the monk could have used.*

The gentleman was so affected by his experience that he wrote to the editor of a local newspaper to find out if anyone had an explanation for the strange occurrence. The following week a reply was printed in the Observer:

*I was returning home late one night using the same pathway, when I was about halfway down I met a man dressed like a monk, in a black robe and wearing sandals. He spoke to me in some outlandish language which I could not understand, and I said so. He repeated his request, but it was no use, I didn't understand him. The monk seemed saddened and turned away. I proceeded on my way, but after a few steps, something made me turn round to have another look at the strange figure, but to my surprise it had disappeared.*

These are just a few of the many sightings of the poor monk of St John's who, hopefully, may one day find peace.

# Crime and Punishment

## A Message from the Dead

*Ouija; A board with letters, signs, etc. used with planchette*
*for obtaining messages in spiritualist seances*
*(French oui yes; German ja yes).*
*A planchette is a small usually heart-shaped board*
*supported by two castors and a pencil, which,*
*when one or more persons rest their fingers lightly on the board,*
*is supposed to write without conscious direction*

The late Ray Mulligan, who was a Chester Blue Badge guide, used to tell this story of the Ouija Board, which to his knowledge was absolutely true:

*In the autumn of 1990 a young man who lived in Tarvin Road had an experience with the supernatural, He had been to visit a friend who was dabbling with a Ouija board. In due course the young man bought a board for himself, on which he frequently experimented.*

*Eventually, as he manipulated his ouija board, certain sequences of letters would keep reappearing. Then, one day, a certain name that seemed familiar to him appeared on the board. A few days later the name returned again. He was elated at the thought that he had gained contact with the dead. However, he also felt very uneasy about it.*

*Nevertheless, he could not resist having another go. The name reappeared whilst he manipulated the board, but this time he felt a strong impulse to visit the medieval Leper Cemetery which was only a few hundred yards away. So he went to the old cemetery.*

*Now, there are only a few gravestones left in this ancient cemetery, most having weathered away or been removed, so searching did not take too long. He read the first and second inscription, and then the third stone and there, staring at him from the grave, was the name from the Ouija.*

*As he read the name on the stone he felt such an evil aura that the hairs stood up on the back of his neck! He felt so terrified that he rushed from the graveyard and back to his home. He entered his house only to find that the evil presence from the graveyard was waiting there for him.As he went into his living room a thick swirling haze coiled about forming different shapes as though to engulf him. In a blind panic to rid himself of the apparition, he* crashed open the back door in the hope that it would blow away. To his dread it made no difference, and the presence just continued to engulf and suffocate him.

Somehow he got out of the house, but looking back he could see that the presence was still waiting for him there. He stumbled his way to the home of his friend and then went to his doctor. In the end they had to call in an exorcist to rid the property of the evil presence!

## The Way of the Sculls

The old leper burial ground in Ray's story is just to the south of the junction between Tarvin and Christleton Roads. It marks the site of St Giles' hospital, founded as a refuge for lepers under the control of St Werburgh's Abbey by Earl Ranulph III of Chester (1181- 1232). There is a local tale that, during the Welsh Wars, one of the Norman earls cobbled (paved) the highway by the graveyard with the bleached skulls of the Welshmen killed in battle. Anyway, the hospital with its chapel is said to have been destroyed during the siege of Chester in 1645. The burial ground was used for victims of the terrible plagues of the 16th and 17th centuries. Because of the presence of the hospital, Boughton was known formerly as Spital (Hospital) Boughton to distinguish it from Great Boughton to the east.

Just a few steps from the graveyard are the reservoirs and water tower of the waterworks. From Roman times onwards, wells and springs at Boughton and Christleton were used to supplement the supply of water available from the River Dee. People have often associated water with the supernatural.

*Boughton water fountain and graveyard mound leper cemetery*

*Photo: Mike Penney*

46

The soldiers of the XXth (20th) Legion, part of the Roman forces which conquered and then occupied Britain for over 400 years, believe in the gods and the supernatural. So they took due care to erect an altar beside the aqueduct which they constructed to carry water from the spring at Boughton to the fortress they were building at Deva (Chester). This they dedicated to *Nymphis et Fontibus* (to nymphs and springs).

**Altar to Nymphs**

Also very close to the old graveyard, to the west of St Paul's Church, is a small public garden overlooking the River Dee that marks the site of Gallows' Hill. Until the beginning of the 19th century, when the Northgate Gaol and later the City Gaol near the Infirmary were used, this was the place of public execution of condemned criminals. This was the scene of the martyrdom of two priests, one an Anglican and the other a Roman Catholic. An obelisk now stands on the site of the two executions.

## Bloody Mary and George Marsh

*Burning was a horrible death,*
*it could take an hour while the legs burned away.*

When the young King Edward VI died, Mary (born 1516, reigned 1553-1558) had to lead a popular uprising to seize the throne from Lady Jane Grey, the

### Boughton obelisk

*Photo: Roy Wilding*

47

nine days' Queen. It was the last popular thing that Mary did. She promised that she would not force Roman Catholicism on the English but did not keep her promise. Just a year into her reign she married the Catholic King Philip of Spain, a marriage so unpopular that it could not take place in London for fear of crowd violence, and was carried out in Winchester instead.

Religious persecution reached new heights. Catholic cardinals were given power and Protestants were burned at the stake. In four years of her reign, 277 men and woman were burned to death, from peasants to bishops such as Hugh Latimer and Thomas Cranmer, the former Archbishop of Canterbury, who held his right hand into the flames, saying that *it should burn first.*

George Marsh, a widower with children, was said to be the only person martyred in Cheshire under Bloody Mary. Marsh was found guilty of heresy and preaching Luther's doctrine in 1554 by the Consistory Court, which at that time was held in the Lady Chapel of the Chester Cathedral. (The Consistory Court is an ecclesiastical court presided over by the chancellor of the diocese. The court furniture from 1635 is now sited in the base of the unfinished south-west tower of the Cathedral.) George Coates, the Bishop of Chester pronounced sentence that Marsh was to *be burned to ashes as a heretic.*

It is said that the room over the Great Abbey Gate, leading to Abbey Square, was used as a prison and that George Marsh was held there for four months. Once or twice sympathizers cast money through a hole in the wall to him.

On 24th April 1555, the sheriffs led him out with his feet shackled *with their officers and great number of poor simple barbers with rusty bills and poleaxes.* He was lead to Gallows' Hill reading his bible. When he arrived Marsh turned to the crowd, but a sheriff said *George Marsh, we must have no sermonizing now.* When the stake was ready, he was offered a pardon by the Vice-Chamberlain on condition that he recant, which he refused.

John Cowper of Overleigh, one of the two sheriffs in that year, took matters into his own hands and attempted to rescue Marsh, but he was held off by Robert Amery, the other sheriff. Cowper fled across the bridge at Holt into Wales, where he hid until Queen Mary's death. His family lost a great deal of their property in consequence. The sheriff's men had great difficulty in lighting the fire and keeping it going, but Marsh is said to have *suffered the agonies with great patience.*

Queen Mary was to die a sad and lonely woman. She loved Philip of Spain, but after the wedding he only visited her once. In her loneliness she had two phantom pregnancies, but, not surprisingly, since her husband was in Spain,

48

bore no children. At Spain's bidding, she made war on France and lost Calais, England's last possession there. *"When I die, you will find Calais engraved on my heart,"* were alleged to be her dying words. She died, of an ovarian cyst, aged 42.

## In the Name of the Father

Cancerous religious hatred festered and infected this island long after Bloody Mary's reign. In 1559 Elizabeth I suppressed the re-founded religious houses, and became Supreme Governor of the English Church. In that year the Act of Uniformity was passed, ordering the use of the 1552 Prayer Book. In 1569, the northern Catholic earls led by the earls of Northumberland and Westmorland, led a revolt in an abortive attempt to restore Roman Catholic worship and release Mary, Queen of Scots from captivity. They ransacked Durham Cathedral, but fled to Scotland when faced with Elizabeth's army.

In 1570 Queen Elizabeth was excommunicated and declared deposed by Pope Pius V and has a result, Catholics come under suspicion as potential traitors. A year later, Roberto di Ridofi, a Florentine, plotted with Philip II, the Duke of Alva and the Pope to marry Mary, Queen of Scots, to the Duke of Norfolk, depose Queen Elizabeth thus restoring Roman Catholicism to England. However the plot was exposed, resulting in the execution of the Duke of Norfolk and the Earl of Westmorland in 1572.

By 1573, fighting in Scotland ended with the Pacification of Perth and, later, the surrender of Edinburgh Castle to an English army, which finally freed Elizabeth I from all threats from Scotland. In addition, support for Mary in Scotland finally collapsed. During the summer of 1580 Edmund Campion and Robert Parsons began a Jesuit mission in England. The following year fear spread in England that a Jesuit invasion was imminent. Also, in 1581, a law was passed that converts to Roman Catholicism in England were subject to high treason.

Francis Throckmorton led a conspiracy in 1583 to overthrow Queen Elizabeth and to free Mary Stuart, however when his plot was discovered he was executed. The following year an *Association of Noblemen* was formed, with the approval of Parliament, *to pursue to the death anyone plotting against the Queen;* it was even signed by Mary.

In 1586, the Babington Plot to kill the Queen was uncovered by Sir Francis Walsingham, and Babington and his fellow conspirators were duly executed. Just over the Welsh border from Chester, at Plas Cadwgan near Wrexham, lived Edward Jones. Jones helped his friend Thomas Salusbury of Llewenny to escape after his part in the plot. Jones was hung, drawn and quartered, and the Crown confiscated Plas Cadwgan. This, for just lending Salusbury a horse.

In the same year Margaret Clitheroe of York suffered horrific execution on being pressed to death for hiding priests. In the year of 1587 Mary, Queen of Scots was executed, for her implication in the Babington Plot to overthrow Queen Elizabeth and restore Roman Catholicism in England, after nearly 19 years in prison.

In 1588, thirty-one Roman Catholic priests were executed in England and the Spanish Armada set sail from Lisbon, but Howard and Drake famously defeated it off Plymouth.

For the rest of the 16th century the Spanish continued to be a threat to England. Then in 1601 two fleets from Spain arrived to help the Irish in their rebellion against English rule. However, 1602 saw Lord Mountjoy capture the invading Spanish army in Ireland. In the same year the Jesuits were ordered to leave England.The Treaty of London was signed in 1604, when Peace was finally declared between Britain and Spain.

## 5th November 1605

*Please to remember the 5th November; Gunpowder Treason and Plot*

To countless generations of English folk the date of 5th November 1605 has been celebrated as a day of deliverance. However, it may not be unreasonable to suggest that had the plot been successful then history would have been drastically changed, just as the modern tragic events of the 11th September 2001 with the destruction of the American World Trade Center have profoundly altered the course of modern history.

In 1604 the Hampton Court Conference met to discuss Church reforms. However, James I disappointed the Puritans by failing to resolve religious conflicts. However, the conference did lead to the production of the Authorized Version of the Bible.

Having failed to gain religious toleration from King James, the Catholics planned to destroy King and Parliament by blowing up the Houses of Parliament when it was in session with the King present. As we all know, the plot was discovered and 36 barrels of gunpowder were found in the cellars of the Houses of Parliament. This was the last major Catholic conspiracy. Some of the conspirators were killed at their headquarters, Holbeach House;

others, including Guy Fawkes, were captured, tortured and then later executed by being hanged, drawn and quartered.

So it was that religious turmoil and unrest simmered and boiled throughout the reign of the Stuart dynasty. Everyone is aware of the catastrophic effects of the policy of the colonization of Ulster by the English in 1611, involving the confiscation of the estates of rebel lords and sharing out among the English and Scottish immigrants, with the subjugation of the Irish people. In addition, the English Civil Wars were an immense turning point in English, if not world, history.

## Non-Conformists

It is little wonder with all these momentous national and international events unfolding that Chester could avoid being unscathed from the troubles. In 1662 two years after the return of the monarchy, in the shape of King Charles II, came the Act of Uniformity and the effect of this Act was that many Nonconformist Puritan and Presbyterian pastors were removed from their churches and forced to bear oppression and hardship. Many Nonconformists were driven away, and amongst others, many Chester citizens immigrated to America with numbers settling at Boston Mass. It is said that many old Chester names can be seen on the signboards and in other places in Boston.

### *Persecution of non-conformists*

However, perhaps the people who suffered most during the time of persecution were the Roman Catholics and particularly their clergy, as it was High Treason to perform the office of the Roman Catholic priest. This may have been the result of the persecutions of Protestants in Bloody Mary's reign,

51

or memories of the Gunpowder Plot. Whatever the cause, the Roman Catholic clergy and others of that faith were much persecuted and often treated with great cruelty.

## Father John Plessington

On the 19th July 1679, the Roman Catholic priest Father John Plessington (canonized in 1979) was executed for High Treason under the Titus Oates Act. (In 1678, Isreal Tonge and Titus Oates had concocted the Popish Plot, which was whipped up by Danby, the Lord High Treasurer. Tongue falsely revealed that in April 1678, Roman Catholic conspirators had plotted to kill the King. Some 35 Catholics were executed as a result of this fraud. Danby was later impeached on a charge of criminal correspondence with France and was dismissed from Office. Titus Oates (1649-1705) was found guilty of perjury in 1685 and condemned and imprisoned, but was released three years later and granted a pension.)

Plessington was drawn to the place of execution upon a hurdle and put to death for high treason by being hanged, and before being quite dead, cut down and the body cut into four quarters. The four quarters were to be hung on the four City Gates (although it is not recorded that this took place in this instance). He his said to have died calling on God to *bless the King and Royal Family.*

**Father Plessington on the hurdle**

## Hung, Drawn and Quartered

This form of execution, more precisely called drawing, hanging and quartering, was one of the most sadistic punishments ever devised.The condemned man was drawn to the place of execution tied to a hurdle (like a piece of fencing from thin branches interwoven to form a panel), that was dragged by a horse.

Once there, the prisoner was hanged without a drop to ensure his neck wasn't broken, and cut down while still conscious. He was disembowelled and finally had his head cut off and his body divided into four quarters. The head and quarters were parboiled to prevent them rotting too quickly and displayed on the city gates as a warning to all.

There are various claims as to when this punishment was first used. One source states that it was specifically invented, in 1241, to execute William Maurice, who had been convicted of piracy; it soon became the stock execution method for men convicted of high treason. Women were burned at the stake, for decency's sake.

Another source has it that King Edward I used it for the first time, when he was at Chester, to execute Dafydd of North Wales. However, it is certain that, in 1399, Piers Leigh was executed in this manner, for supporting Richard II, and his head was then placed on Chester castle tower. In 1587, a man was hanged, drawn and quartered and the quarters stuck on the four Chester gates, for the crime of clipping money.

Drawing, hanging and quartering remained the lawful punishment for treason until 1814, when the part of the sentence relating to disembowelling was altered to hanging until death supervened. Drawing and beheading and quartering after hanging were officially abolished in 1870, having long fallen into disuse.

There is some debate as to who was the last person to receive this punishment. Some cite five of the Cato Street conspirators, who planned to assassinate the Cabinet and seize power in 1820. However, most contemporary accounts say they were simply hanged.

The Pentrich Revolution, a peasants revolt of 1817, saw the ringleaders William Turner, Jeremiah Brandreth and Isaac Ludlum sentenced to drawing, hanging and quartering. They were probably the last to receive this punishment on November 7th 1817.

## *Dead Man Hanging*

The last three public executions on Gallows' Hill took place on 9th May 1801; two forgers Samuel Thompson and John Morgan; and the third was a handsome young man in his twenties named John Clare, who had been convicted of a relatively minor burglary. John Clare created interest on receiving his sentence by loudly declaring that he would never hang.

On the day of execution, when the three men were led from the cart that took them to the gallows, the crowd pushed forward to get a better view and this gave John Clare the chance he had been waiting for. He pulled the ropes off his wrists and, despite wearing heavy leg irons, made a desperate bid for freedom. The crowd drew back in surprise, allowing Clare through. He fell, staggered to his feet, then fell once more. This time he rolled down the steep high bank towards the river Dee below. The crowd scrambled after him, greatly impeding the sheriffs men. Clare plunged into the swollen waters, and hopelessly attempted to swim to the Handbridge bank and safety. He could only manage a few yards when, pulled down by his leg irons, the poor young man drowned.

*Hanging man        Bewick woodcut*

It took an hour for the sheriffs' men to find his body and drag it out of the river. Their next dreadful action horrified the crowd, although the crowd had come

54

eagerly expecting to witness death, they were not prepared for the sight of John Clare's corpse being dragged to the scaffold. They watched in dread as the noose was placed around the dead man's neck, and his corpse swung from the gallows. The two forgers, Thompson and Morgan, were forced to stand in terror and watch these gruesome events until their fate finally came. However, this was not the last of the day's macabre events, for while the bodies were being transported back to the prison for burial the bad condition of the road and the incompetence of the driver caused the cart to overturn in Pepper Street. The three corpses, two of which were still warm, were flung into the road for all to see. John Clare's body was still soaking wet.

## The Moral of Ray's Story

So the area around the old cemetery has a terrible track record of death, violence and destruction and it is no surprise that when the young man in Ray's story dabbled into the supernatural that something awful would happen, - in this case the manifestation of a smoke ghost.

## The Northgate Gaol

The present Northgate replaced an earlier gate in 1810. Until 1807 the gatehouse of the previous Northgate was used as the infamous city jail.

*The old North Gate of the city*

The contemporary historian Hemingway described it as *"An inconvenient and unseemly pile of buildings"*. Both the gate and the jail were under the control of the city sheriffs. Parts of the jail were excavated from the rock below the wall. Descriptions of it in the 17th century refer to a dark stinking place called *'dead men's room'* where prisoners who had been condemned to death were confined.

There was also another cell called 'Little Ease', which was about 1.5 meters high and about half a meter at its greatest in width and depth. It was said that the height could be lessened, as a form of torture, by fixing wooden boards across the cell. Shortly before the jail was demolished, the jailer reported that he found an iron glove used for restraining uncooperative prisons.

Adjacent to the Northgate and just a few yards to the west of the road bridge which runs high over the canal is a slender, narrow and dangerous looking stone footbridge that links the walls and the Bluecoat building. Known as the Bridge of Sighs, this bridge, which originally had iron railings, was built in 1793 as a means of securing a link between the jail and Little St John's chapel, where there was an *apartment made for the prisoners*. In popular tradition it is said that condemned felons used it to receive their last rights at the chapel, before they came back to execution by the drop where their bodies were dropped and hanged in front of the crowd.

**Bridge of Sighs**

# Horrible Executions at Chester

In the early part of the 19th century, the Chester historian Hemingway made a record of some of the executions that had taken place at Chester between 1554 and 1829. The following list has been left in Hemingway's own words, because it gives a good idea about contemporary brutal attitudes towards crime and punishment in those days.

1558 - A woman burnt at Boughton for poisoning her husband.
1589 - John Taylor, gaoler of the castle, for murder of Mr. Hockenhall, a prisoner in his custody for recusancy (refusal to attend Church of England church services).
1592 William Geaton, servant to the bishop of Chester, for the murder of James Findlove, a Scottish pedlar; his body was hung in chains on Groppenhall (Grappenhall) heath.

1601 A woman named Candy, executed for conspiring to murder her husband; her paramour, Boon, refusing to plead, was pressed to death in the castle.
1602 One Arnet, servant to a Mr. Manley, of Saltney side, hung for murdering his fellow-servant.
1654 Sir Timothy Fetherstone, shot in the corn-market of Chester, by order of the Parliament.

1750 Two Irishmen executed, and gibbeted on the Parkgate Road, near the two mills, for murder.
1768 Three men hung: the rope of one of them broke, when lifting up his cap, he exclaimed in horrible agitation, "My God! What am I to suffer?"
1776 Execution of James Knight, for burglary at Odd Rode.
    Christopher Lawless, Isaac Hutcinson, Alexander Solomon, and Isaac Josephs, executed for robbing the shop of Mr. Pemberton, jeweller. They were buried behind the Roodee-cop, opposite Overleigh.
1777 S. Thorley, executed for the horrible murder of Ann Smith, a ballad-singer, near Congleton. After cutting off her head, he severed her legs and arms from her body, which he threw into a brook! Part, however, he actually broiled and ate! He was hung in chains on the heath, near Congleton.
1779 William Ellis for burglary, and William Loom, discharging a loaded pistol at Charles Warren, of Congleton, executed at Boughton.
1779 Sarah Jones, executed for stealing 28 yards of chintz, from the shop of Mr. Meacock, at Chester.
1783 Resolution Heap, and Martha Brown; the former a burglary at Whaley; the latter for a similar offence at Over.
1784 Elizabeth Wood, hung for poisoning James Sinister, at Bredbury.
    John Oakes, hung for coining (forging).
1786 Executions of Peter Steers, for the murder of his wife, by poison.
    Edward Holt, for a burglary at Knutsford.
    Thomas Buckley, age 20, for a burglary at Chester. Thomas Hyde, aged 35, for horse-stealing.
    James Buckley, aged 22, for a burglary in Mrs. Lloyd's house in Newgate Street,

Chester.

1789  Thomas Mate, for the murder of John Parry, a constable, in Handbridge. He was 64 years old, and when at the gallows, he charged his wife, 70 years old, with infidelity.
1790  John Dean, from Stockport, for the most brutal murder of his wife, who was seven months advanced in her pregnancy. He was hung in chains on Stockport moor.
1791  Execution of Lowndes, for robbing the Warrington mail. His prosecution, it is said, cost £2,000. He was hung in chains on Helsby Hill; but the gibbet pole was in short time after cut down by some people in the neighbourhood, and was not again erected.

Allen, Aston, and Knox, for burglary at Northern. Upon this occasion, the fatal tree was removed from Gallows hill to the opposite side of the road, where it remained until 1801, when the place of execution was finally removed within the walls of the city.

*Gallows Hill*  Bewick woodcut (altered)

1796  Thomas Brown and James Price, for robbing the Warrington mail. They were hung in chains on Trafford-green, and remained there till 1820, when the pole was taken down, the place having been previously enclosed. In the skull of Price was found a robin's nest.
1798  John Thornhill, for the murder of his sweetheart, Sarah Malone, at Lymm.
Peter Martin, alias Joseph Lowther, for firing at a boat's crew of the Actaon, in the Mersey, when employed on the impress service.

1800  Thomas Bosworth, for forgery, and Alexander Morton, for felony.
Mary Lloyd for forgery at Stockport.
1801  Thompson, Morgan, and Clare, for burglaries. When near the gallows, Clare made a spring from the cart, rushed through the crowd, which made way for him, rolled down a gutter-way towards the Dee a rapid descent and plunged into the river. He was drowned, having immediately sunk, from the weight of his chains, but the body was found, and afterwards hung up with the others, the other two malefactors being kept in the cart in the interval. These were the last criminals hung at Boughton, which had been the place of execution for some centuries.
1801  Aaron Gee and Thomas Gibson, hung out of a temporary window way, in the

58

attics, on the south side of the old Northgate, a building now not in existence. The unfortunate men were propelled from the window about five feet (about one and a half meters), and dropped nearly forty inches (just over one meter), their bodies beating against the window beneath, so as to break the glass in them.

1809 Execution of George Glover and William Proudlove, in front of the house of correction, for shooting at an officer of excise at Odd Rode. When the drop sunk, the ropes broke, and the poor men fell to the platform, half-strangled; new ropes were procured, and the sentence was carried into effect about an hour after the incident.

1810 Execution of John Done, for the murder of Betty Eckersley, a woman of bad character, at Lymm. He denied the offence to his last moment.

Executions of Smith and Clark, for a burglary and felony in the shop of Mr. Fletcher, a watch-maker, East Gate. The conduct of Smith on the drop was exceedingly unbending and audacious, and the night before his execution he played at cards with some of his companions. They were buried in St. Martin's churchyard.

1812 Temple and Thompson for rioting. They were connected with the Luddites.

Execution of John Lomas, for the murder of his master, Mr. Morrey, of Hankelow.

1813 Edith Murrat, executed for the murder of her husband. She was tried with Lomas, and with him found guilty on the clearest testimony. Immediately after conviction she pleaded pregnancy, and a jury of matrons being impannelled, she was pronounced quick with child, and her sentence of course respited till her delivery. It appeared that an illicit intercourse had for some time existed between her and Lomas, which led her to exciting him to destroy her husband, and the crime was perpetrated with circumstances of peculiarly savage atrocity.

1813 Execution of William Wilkinson, James Yarwood, and William Burgess, for rape on Mary Porter, near Weston Point. They were flat-men (flatboats are a type of boat), and when Wilkinson (a fine stout man about six feet high) mounted the scaffold, he exclaimed to his companions, "Keep your spirits; never mind, my lads we are all murdered men; I'm just as happy as if I was going to a play!" and when the halter was placed round his neck, he added, "My new handkerchief fits me nice and tight."

1814 William Wilson, an old sailor, in his 70th year, executed for arson, at Tiverton, near Tarporley. His exit was most extraordinary: on the morning of his death he entertained a number of persons in the parlour of the constables house, with an account of his naval exploits; and in his way along the streets to the city gaol he chewed bread in his mouth, and threw it at the beadle, observing he was like Peeping Tom at Coventry. On the drop he said, "What a many people are here to see an old man hung; here's as much fuss as if there were a hundred to be hanged.

1815 Execution of Griffith and Wood, for burglary in the house of John Holme, near Stockport.

1817 Execution of Joseph Allen, for uttering bank of England notes to a large amount. In a declaration on the morning of the execution, he said he had been wrongly accused, and that he did not know good notes from bad ones. For six days after his condemnation, he took no other refreshment than water.

1818 Abraham Rostern and Isaac Moors, the former for a burglary at Edgeley, the latter for a similar offence at Cheadle Bulkeley. Both of them acknowledged their guilt.

1819 Joseph Walker, for robbing his former master on the highway between Northwich and Manchester. He denied his guilt to the last.

Samuel Hooley and John Johnson (a man of colour) for burglary at Bowden.

1820  Jacob McGhinnes, for shooting Mr. Birch, at Stockport. He was connected with the radical reformers, and his intention was to have shot Mr. Lloyd, then solicitor of the town, and now notable prothonotary of the county court. The unfortunate man had not only embraced the politics both the theology of Tom Pain, but during his confinement, and before his execution, he was brought to embrace the Christian system and died with great composure.

Thomas Miller, for a burglary at Bowden. Ralph Ellis, for a burglary at Elton.

And William Ricklington, for setting fire to the rectory house at Coddington.

1821  Execution of Samuel Healey, for highway robbery at Stockport.

1822  William Tongue for rape on an infant, and George Groom for a highway robbery on a man named Joseph Kennerly.

Thomas Brierly, for highway robbery near Congleton.

1823  Execution of Samuel Fallows, for the murder of his sweetheart. Several galvanic experiments were made on his body previous to dissection.

Execution of John Kragon, for rape of an infant at Stockport.

Execution of Edward Clark, for a highway robbery at Stockport.

1824  Joseph Dale, for the murder of Mr. Wood, near Disley. He had been convicted at the preceding assizes, but execution deferred, in order to take the opinion on a point of law urged in his favour by Mr. D.F. Jones, his counsel. He died with great composure.

1826  Philip McGowan, for the robbery of Mr. Marsden, a gentleman of upwards of seventy \years of age, near Cowlane-bridge, under circumstances of great violence.
On this melancholy occasion, the apparatus for execution, was removed from the east to the west end of the city gaol, where these melancholy spectacles have ever since been  exhibited.

John Green, for burglary.

1829  John Proudlove, for highway robbery, and John Leir, for burglary in the house of the Rev. Matthew Bloor, attended with aggravated circumstances of violence.

Joseph Woodhouse, for a rape on his own daughter; and Joseph Henshall, for firing a gun at the keepers, while poaching in the ground of the Earl of Stamford and Warrington.

*Bewick woodcut*

## In Suspicious Circumstances

Even as late as Victorian times there were over two hundred crimes for which the penalty was death.Large crowds would enjoy going to see public executions and treat it as an enjoyable day out! I can remember my grand father, born in Chester in 1871, telling about my great grandfather recalling how he went to see the executions and that people took very young children along and lifted them up to get a better view!

*Preparing the noose*

*Bewick woodcut*

The last female public hanging, in Chester, took place on December 28th 1863, when Alice Hewitt, of Handbridge, was hung for poisoning her mother for the insurance money. The Alice Hewitt case was featured in the actor Edward Woodward's television crime series: 'In Suspicious Circumstances'. The execution took place at the City Jail, the present site of the Queen's School.

## The Old Rocking Chair

The last male public hanging, in Chester, took place on 23rd April 1866, when Samuel Griffiths was hung for murder, also at the City Jail. By a strange coincidence, the murder by Samuel Griffiths could be linked to a ghost story that my mother used to tell me over 50 years ago. Bertha Dodd, my mother, was born in the village of Barrow by Chester in 1901, and the Dodd family was one of only four families recorded to have lived there for hundreds of years.The Dodds then lived in an ancient thatched cottage in Long Green, called Rose Cottage.

My mother recalled how a rickety old rocking chair, that stood by the window of the cottage would, particular on a warm summer's evening, gently rock all by itself. The family believed that it was the spirit of an elderly person rocking in the chair, and they (the Dodds) neither minded nor bothered about it. My mother didn't seem to be aware of any violent events connected with the cottage, although she did say that it had burnt down several times over the generations.

Oddly, when researching for this book, I was surprised to learn of the brutal murder by Samuel Griffiths in February 1866 of Isaac Newport, of Rose Cottage, Long Green, Barrow. Isaac was 65 years old, kept a smallholding, and was a member of one of Barrow's oldest and respected families (There is a full account of the murder in the Chester Record issues for March 1866). Griffiths confessed to murdering poor Isaac for the £14.7s he had on him:

He (Griffiths) said simply that he was in the Railway Inn, and when he saw the money paid by Mrs Lightfoot (farmer) to Newport, he determined to have it. He followed and caught him (Newport) at the bottom of Woodlands field, where he knocked him down and took the money. The old man got up and begged for £5 back, but he refused. For a while they walked on together and crossed the stile into the 'Christian field' where he decided to kill Newport so that he would not report on him. Three or four times he hit him in the face with his fist and pushed him into the ditch. He was, however, still alive so he held his head under the water in the ditch and within a minute he was dead.

Griffiths was known to be a terror in the neighbourhood on account of his pilfering and rowdy habits. He was 26 years old, and had lived in Dunham since he was 13. He had previously served time in both Chester and Knutsford jails.

The trial was held before Mr Justice Blackburn in Chester on 5th April 1866. At this time the Cattle Plague was raging throughout Cheshire, and Griffiths had been employed in killing and burying cows near the Christian Field. The accused was found guilty of murder and sentence to hang. The execution was to take place in the presence of the High Sheriff, Mr Robert Barbour of Bolesworth Castle.

The execution took place during Chester Race Week in April 1866. A short time before 7 'clock a grey-headed man in a white smock, who was Smith, the Hangman, arranged a black cloth in front of the drop. At around 8 o'clock there was a crowd of about 2,000 people gathered, who behaved very orderly. The gallows had been erected over the gateway of the jail, and Griffith prayed with a white cap over his head as he walked to the scaffold. The scaffold's bolt was drawn, and Griffiths body dropped and was left hanging for one hour, then cut down, and buried in the jail. The last public execution in England took place outside Newgate Prison, London on 25th May 1868.

It would be nice to think that good and honest old Isaac, so cruelly murdered, found peace and comfort in his rickety old rocking chair.

# In the Executioner's Graveyard

## St. Mary-on-the-Hill

St. Mary-on-the-Hill's medieval graveyard is only separated from Chester Castle by a deep ditch and, because of its close proximity to the castle, was naturally used for the burial of prisoners who had been condemned to death at the Assizes held in the castle. There are therefore many entries in the Registers of St. Mary's showing how common these executions were. Some of the entries are particularly macabre:

## Pressed to Death

*1616 Tymothie Tatton, a prisoner, buried ...July. (In the margin, pressed to death).*
*1627 Prisoner pressed, William Wilson, ...April.*
*1631 Thomas Laceby, a prisoner, pressed to death, buried in the churchyard on the north side [of] the steeple the 23rd day of April.*

These entries record just a few of the instances of prisoners suffering the terrible execution of being *pressed to death.* If a prisoner refused to plead he saved what property he had from being forfeited to the Crown, but he had to undergo a special and terrible form of punishment. He was stripped naked and laid on his back in a cellar, with his arms and legs stretched out. A board was placed across his body, and on this was piled up weights and stones *as much as he could bear and more,* and these remained on him until he volunteered to plead or till death released him from his sufferings.

On the first day he was allowed *three morsels of barley without drink,* and on the second day, *two drinks of stagnant (not running) water, without any bread:* and as the judge said, when he decreed this penalty, *this shall be his diet until he is dead.* The duration of this punishment depended on the strength of the prisoner, and in some cases it is known to have lasted from Saturday until the following Monday night, or more than forty-eight hours.

## Three Witches Sleep by the Castle Ditch

*1656. Three witches hanged at Michaelmas Assizes, buried in the corner by the Castle Ditch in Churchyard, 15th or 18th October (there is some doubt about the actual date they were buried).*

The three witches were Ellen, wife of John Beech, of Rainow, near

Macclesfield; Anne, the wife of James Osboston, also of Rainow; and Anne Thornton, of Eaton, near Chester;

At the Session held on the last day of March 1656, Beech and Osboston were accused:

*That Ellen, wife of John Beech, late of Ranowe, in Cheshire, collier, on the 12th September, 1651, and on divers other days as well before as after, at Ranowe, did exercise and practice the Invocation and conjuracon of evil and wicked spirits, and consulted and convenated with, entertayned, employed, ffed and rewarded certayn evill and wicked spirits. On the said 12th day of September the said Ellen Beech did exercise certain Witchcrafts upon Elizabeth Cowper, late of Ranowe, spinster, whereby she, from the 12th till the 20th of September, aforesaid, did languish, and upon the said 20th day died.*

*Anne, the wife of James Osboston, late of Ranowe, in Cheshire, husbandman, on the 12th day of September, 1651, practised certain wicked and divellish acts upon John Steenson, late of Ranowe, husbandman, which caused his death on the 20th of September.*
*The said Anne Osboston on the 20th November 1653, at Ranowe exercised certayn artes and Incantacons on Barbara Pott, late wife of John Pott, of Ranowe, from the effects whereof she died on the 20th of January then next following.*
*And again on the 17th day of July, 1655, the said Anne Osboston practised sorceries on one John Pott, late of Ranowe, yeoman, from which time he languished until the 5th of August, when he died.*
*On the 30th of November, 1651, the said Anne Osboston used enchantments upon Anthony Booth, late of Macclesfield, in the county of Chester, gent. thereby causing his death on the 1st of April then next following.*

Beech and Osboston next appeared at the Sessions held at Chester on the 6th October 1656, and the Justices then *instantly demand how the said Ellen Beech and Anne Osboston will acquit themselves of the premises above charged severally against them.*

Beech and Osboston pleaded not guilty to the charges against them, but the jurors found them both guilty, and they were *sentenced to be hanged severally by their necks.*

Anne Thornton also appeared at the Sessions held on the 6th October 1656, also accused of witchcraft and murder:

*That Ann Thornton, late of Eyton in Cheshire, widow, on the 9th day of February, 1655 (-6), and on divers other days and times, as well before as since, at Eccleston, not having God before her eyes, but by the instigacon of the Devill being moved and seduced [did] with force and arms wickedly, divellishly, and feloniously diverse [devise] exercise and practise certayne divellish and wicked actes and Incantacons called Witchcrafts, Inchauntments, Charmes, and Sorceries in and upon one Daniell ffinchett, sonne of Raphe ffinchett, of Eccleston, yeoman, being an infant of the age of three dayes, whereby he, the said Daniel from the 9th day of February in the year aforesaid until the 11th day of the same month, did languish, upon which 11th day he the aforesaid Daniel by the said wicked and devillish Actes soe by her the aforesaid Ann Thornton used, exercised and practised, as aforesaid, upon him the said Daniel, dyed.*

Anne Thornton pleaded not guilty to the charges, but sadly, she also was found guilty and sentenced to hang. John Bradshaw*, for the Lord Protector (Cromwell), demanded that the three women be executed at Boughton on Wednesday the 15th October, at about three oclock in the afternoon.
The sentences were duly carried out and the women were buried either on the 15th or 18th October 1656.

*This was John Bradshaw, of Congleton, the Attorney-General for the County Palatine of Chester, and not John Bradshaw, the Chief Justice of Chester, one of the regicides of King Charles I.

From around 1560 to 1675, many prosecutions of so-called witches took place in England and Wales. Most trials involved old women, usually widows, which were not only based on the ignorant belief that the poor accused was a real witch, but sometimes on trumped up charges just to depose of her.

Witchcraft laws were passed in 1604 under James I, who was paranoid about witches and witchcraft, and whose *Demonology* became the standard reference work for witchcraft trails. Witches could be executed for inflicting bodily harm, calling or *conjuring up* spirits and demons, stealing corpses, and murder.

Horrific methods were inflicted to try to prove a witch's guilt. *Pricking* involved piercing the accused's bodily marks with a needle or bodkin to find the *Devil's mark,* which was believed to be immune from pain and bleeding. This process could be repeated numerous times until an insensitive, bloodless mark was found. Prickers could earn high fees, and would go to extreme lengths to find the mark of guilt. Once this was found, the bodkin was inserted down to the bone and if there was no pain or blood, the case was proved.

In 1612, the Pendle, in Lancashire, witch trials were held. One of the ten condemned women was accused of murdering Robert Nutter, who died in

Chester in 1596 and was a retainer of Sir Richard Shuttleworth, Chief Justice of Chester. Ten years earlier, an alleged witch was tried in Chester. Margery Kendall, wife of David Kendall, a labourer, was charged with practising witchcraft on Joan Eaton, until she was in danger of her life. Margery had been previously indicted as a common scold, but her conviction on a charge of witchcraft is not recorded.

Chester's other known witchcraft trial was in 1663, when Elizabeth Powell, widow, was charged by Thomas Annion, blacksmith, with felony upon suspicion of witchcraft. Felony was a serious crime, for which land or goods could be forfeited. It may be that Annion attempted to obtain Powell's property by falsely accusing her of witchcraft. Elizabeth Powell was sent to the Northgate Gaol, where she died in 1669 after a long illness.

## For Whom the Bell Tolls

As if to prove that Death has no bias, an entry in the register shows the burial of one of the men who, no doubt, helped many a poor prisoner out of this world:

*1643 John Edwards, Hangman,
buried in north churchyard 17th of November.*

*Bewick Woodcut*

# A
# JOURNAL
### OF THE
## 𝕻𝖑𝖆𝖌𝖚𝖊 𝕿𝖊𝖆𝖗𝖘
### BEING
## Obſervations or Memorials,
#### Of the moſt Remarkable
# OCCURRENCES,
#### As well
# PUBLICK *as* PRIVATE,
#### Which happened in
# *CHESTER*
#### During the laſt
# GREAT VISITATION

---

## By Roy Wilding

---

*CHESTER.*

# Plague

## Bubonic Plague

The bubonic plague that hit Chester in 1665 was the final assault of a disease that is now part of the folklore of medieval and renaissance Europe. One contemporary eye-witness leaves a terrible account of the plague, in the form of a note in the register of the parish church of St Mary-on-the-Hill, Chester:

*The plague takes them very strangely, strikes them black on the one side and then they run mad, some drown themselves, others would kill themselves, they dye within [a] few hours, some run up and down in the streets in their shirts to the great horror of those in the city.*

Daniel Defoe, in *A Journal of the Plague Year*, describes graphically how the physicians and doctors of that time tortured many poor sufferers to death:

*The pain of the swelling was in particular very violent, and to some intolerable; The swellings in some grew hard, and they (the doctors) applied violent drawing-plaisters or poultices to break them, and if these did not do they cut and scarified them in a terrible manner... then they burnt them with caustics, so that many died raving mad with the torment, and some in the very operation.*

Contemporary doctors had no idea how to cure the plague. The real cause of the disease was not identified until the 19th century, when scientists discovered that fleas transmitted the bacteria from infected rats to man. However, at the time, it was believed that the disease was the result of sin or that it was carried by 'miasma', the vapours given off by rotting matter.

The disease manifested itself in buboes, dark swellings about the size of a hens egg in the armpits, groin or neck. The Plague, also known as bubonic plague, pestis, and the Black Death had, in Chester, a local name: 'Stubbs Bile'. It was an acute, severe infection caused by the bacillus *Yersinia pestis*. The bacillus is primarily an internal parasite of wild rodents, such as rats, mice and squirrels. It is carried to man by rat fleas *Xenopsylla cheopis* deserting dying or dead animals in search of nourishment.

It is often assumed that survivors of the plague had suffered the bubonic form. However *Pestis Minor*, a benign form of bubonic plague has been identified as occurring alongside bubonic plague in (modern) epidemic areas. The signs and symptoms of *Pestis Minor* are similar to that of bubonic plague but subside within a week.

# Pneumonic Plague

Another, even more deadly, strand of the disease was pneumonic plague. This attacked the lungs and was spread by coughs and sneezes, hence the grisly nursery rhyme 'Ring-A-Ring-Roses':

*The ring of roses described the purple rash which developed, the pocket full of posies referred to the herbs used to try to ward off the disease, while A-tish-oo showed that the infection was spread by coughs and sneezes.*

It had a two to three day incubation period that was followed by an abrupt onset of high fever, chills and often a severe headache. Coughing developed within 12 hours, rapidly developing blood spotting and then acquiring a uniform, bright red, often foamy appearance. Most victims died within 48 hours.

# The Sweat

The *Sweat was* another dreadful disease that swept through Europe. It had many names and was known as The Sweat, The Swat, New Acquaintance, Stoupe, or Knave know thy master. It was claimed that it only killed the rich, middle aged, not the young or the old, and that death came quickly. A priest wrote, *"They were dancing in court at nine and dead at eleven".*

Henry VIII's physician compared it to *the plague at Athens, a pestilent contagious fever of one natural day.* He described the symptoms as:

*"...burning heat, sickness, headache, delirium, intense thirst, laboured breathing, erratic pulse, followed by faintness, drowsiness, profuse sweating, sickness of stomach and heart but seldom vomiting".*

# The Plague of Justinian

The Black Death, in its original form, was bubonic plague, which is native to third world countries such as Uganda, Western Arabia, Kurdistan, Northern India and the Gobi Desert. From time to time it erupts there in the form of minor, localised epidemics. On rare occasions, it breaks out as one of the great pandemics. Bubonic plague, unlike influenza, was thought to move slowly, taking ten years or more to run its course across the world. When it arrives, it stays a long time. Even today, it has not really gone away.

The first pandemic began in Arabia, reached Egypt in the year 542 AD. It devastated and, perhaps, even fatally weakened the Roman Empire of

Justinian. It is said to have travelled across Europe to Britain, where it was known as the *Plague of Cadwaladers Time* or *yellow plague*. In 664 AD, there was a total eclipse of the sun in England, which was feared to be a bad omen, and a *great pestilence ravaged the country.*

Over the centuries there has always been much confusion in identifying true bubonic plague. It was once thought the British epidemic could not have been bubonic plague, because there was no evidence that the house-rat, also known as the black-rat or ship's-rat (from which bubonic plague stems) existed in Britain or Ireland earlier than late 11th to 12th century AD.

However, in 1979, archaeologists found skeletal remains of black rats (*Rattus rattus*) in a late Roman well in York. With this discovery, it is clear that the black rat had entered Britain much earlier than once thought, by at least the 4th century AD. In addition, excavations carried out in the City of London in 1983, have provided further conclusive proof of the presence of the black rat in Roman Britain.

## Sergeant Death

**Tarot card**

*And I looked, and behold a pale horse: and his name that sat on him was Death, and hell followed him.*

The second pandemic, bubonic plague, was called the *Black Death*. The hell that followed Death was starvation, murder, terror, and the breakdown of the medieval system. The Black Death was an unparalleled human disaster. Over the following three hundred years, it would return time after time, only relenting in the second half of the 17th century.

The Black Death originated in central Asia, early in the 14th century. In the autumn of 1347, it had reached the shores of the eastern Mediterranean. It spread across Western Europe in 1348 and struck the shores of England in August of that year. Throughout May 1349 and into the first two weeks of June it struck down priest after priest in Warwickshire and Staffordshire.

It was not until mid-June that it took any significant toll among clergy in Chester. The peak of the epidemic in Chester was in the early part of August 1349. Both the abbot of St Werburgh's Abbey and the prioress of St Mary's Priory died within a short time of each other. Things were so bad, that it was impossible to find anyone able and willing to hold the 'eyre of the forest'. The Old Dee Bridge at Chester remained out of repair for several months, a victim of depopulation by the plague.

It is almost certain that the plague killed at least one third of the population of Chester between 1349 and 1350. All across England and Wales villages were deserted and, in towns and cities, cemeteries were unable to provide graves for the dead. The population was halved in some places. As land became plentiful, rents fell and wages rose. Violence and crime spiralled and travel became dangerous. Interruption of food, supplies and goods added hunger and loss to the agonies of a people already overcome by the grief and menace of the vilest of enemies. In England, the manorial system collapsed, climaxing in the Peasants' Revolt of 1381.

## *Winners & Losers*

Whether fully qualified or not, priests in the plague's shadow were in short supply, and were able to charge highly for their services. In 1350, it was claimed that:

*Priests now refuse to take on the cure of souls... and apply themselves instead to the celebration of commemorative masses and other private office...and they claim greater profits for themselves than those who have the cure of souls.*

Priests that survived the plague were not the only winners. Increasing bargaining power which the Black Death put into the hands of surviving tenants is illustrated by the case of the manor of Rudheath, not far from Chester:

*In money remitted to the tenants ...by the justices of Chester and others, by the advice of the Lord, for the third part of their rent, by reason of the plague which had been raging, because the tenants there wished to depart and leave the holdings on the Lords land unless they obtain this remission until the world do come better again, and the holdings possess a greater value....*

However, there were far more losers than winners:

71

*Encumbered by the necessity of burying their dead at Sandbach (not far from Chester), the parishioners of Goostrey experienced serious inconveniences during the excessive mortality of 1349. Corpses of the plague-victims were left to rot at the roadside...so great were the perils and hazards of the way...*

## The Jonah

In 1507 the city was visited by the sweating sickness; ninety-one householders died in three days *and all but four of them widows*. The summer of 1517 had been very hot, and a violent outbreak of plague had such a terrible effect on everyday life that *grass grew a foot high at the market cross and other parts of the city*. This epidemic may have been the third incident of the sweating sickness, which also attacked London in the September of that year, and drove King Henry VIII from his capital.

The Mayor of Chester, Edmund Gee, died suddenly of the sweating sickness in his year of office in 1550/51, *He came in health from the Pentice and dyed on the night, and dyvers others died of it, forty in one day and night.* Gee seems to have been a bit of a Jonah, because when he was mayor of Liverpool in 1548, there was an epidemic that killed nearly a quarter of the population of that city.

## Buried Alive

Bubonic plague was active in England in 1558, but Chester appears to have been only mildly attacked by it, *few died, but many fled to escape the same [plague]*.

It was common practice that rich people would evacuate the city at the first hint of the disease to the safety of their country retreats. They abandoned their servants, who were totally dependent on them for their survival. Generally, ordinary people, such as tradesmen and labourers, had no option but to stay, because there was nowhere else for them to go. All trade and commerce ceased, with the exception of food trades such as bakers and butchers, and shipping came to a standstill. During times of plague, the population became unemployed. However, the Assembly would find dangerous work for them connected with the plague.

The year 1574 saw a terrible visitation of plague to Chester. By this time it was common practice to try to control the spread of plague by imprisoning both the sick and healthy together in their homes by *Shutting up of the House*. This was the equivalent of being buried alive:

*... where several inmates are in one and the same house, and any person in that house happens to be infected, no other person or family of such house shall be suffered to remove him or themselves without a certificate from the examiners of health of that parish.*

When a case of plague was recorded, the household, as was customary, was shut up, the healthy confined with the infected, to prevent the spread of the disease. Windows were boarded up and doors padlocked from the outside, so that the occupants could not make their escape using duplicate keys. To warn people:

*... every house visited be marked with a red cross of a foot long in the middle of the door, evident to be seen, and with these usual printed words, that is to say, Lord, have mercy upon us, to be set close over the same cross, there to continue until lawful opening of the same house.*

## Freedom!

Shutting-up was virtually a death warrant, so many tried to escape as best they could. They would avoid informing the authorities of an outbreak of plague, thus allowing time to make an escape, before the house was shut-up. Men made unemployed by the plague became *Watchers*, ensuring that people did not get out of their shut-up homes. However, many made their escape through rear windows and doors. The watchers or watchmen also had the duty *to apprehend and take up all night-walkers.... Found within their watch, and bring them to the justice of peace.* The justice of the peace would then decide what further action, if any, should be taken against them, including imprisonment in the Northgate Gaol.

Some residents of Pepper Street complained to the Assembly that shutting-up orders were being ignored:

*...That where it have pleased God to infect divers persons of the same (Pepper) Street with the plague, and where also for avoiding of further infection your worships have taken order that all such so in infected should observe certain good necessary orders by your worships made and provided. But so it is, right worships, that none of the said persons infected do observe any of the orders by your worships in that case taken, to the great danger and peril...*

During the plague of 1602/03, a complaint was made to the mayor that a shoemaker, named Richard Bennet, had abandoned two children to avoid being shut-up:

73

*...that the house of Richard Bennet shoemaker is infected with the plague and forasmuch as it is well known that diverse of that family have removed themselves to shun the infection without comandment or warrant unto a house at Cockfight Hill (probably at the top of Souters Lane) and this withstanding two children of the said Bennet and two of his servants do yet remain in the said Bennet's house in the city.*

*It is ordered that all persons w'ch yet remain in the same house should be by the Constables of the Eastgate presently removed out of the said house and conveyed into the said house at Cockfight Hill unto their said father and mother...*

The document goes on to state that if Bennet refused to take the children, then he would be *punished and compelled to receive them.*

## The Dog Warden

The mayor, Sir John Savage, and the Assembly brought in several other measures to try to control the spread of the disease. Swine were not to be kept in the city, and *no dung, muck nor filth, at any times hereafter be cast, within the walls of the said city,* both on pain of fine or imprisonment.

The Assembly banned the transportation of packs of goods or wares from any other place entering the city, until they had first been opened and *aired without the liberties of the said city,* also on pain of fine or imprisonment.

Dogs were not allowed to leave their owners premises and wander about Chester. Any dog found loose would be killed and their owners punished. Obviously, these measures were totally counterproductive, as the dogs could help to control the black rat, a vital link in the spread of plague. There were strict regulations about receiving strangers into the city, especially from highly suspect places. In 1574, Roger Calcot was bound by the Assembly not to receive any lodgers in his house from London or Bristol.

## Searchers

Plague doctors and *Searchers* found much work in times of plague. Doctors wore ghoulish-looking garb, and the outlandish dress was actually thought to serve as protection:

*The strange, bird-like figure stepped out of the gloom and walked down the dark alleyway. Wearing a beak-like mask filled with aromatic herbs to disguise the stench that hung in the air, the apothecary looked like a monstrous raven.*

74

Searchers were old women paid to go into properties to find corpses:

*That there be a special care to appoint women searchers in every parish... and these to be sworn to make due search and true report to their utmost of their knowledge whether the persons whose bodies they are appointed to search do die of the infection, or of what other disease, as near as they can...*

*That no searcher during this time of visitation be permitted to use any public work or employment, or keep any shop or stall, or be employed as a laundress or in any other common employment whatsoever.*

**Beaked Physician**

Searchers were supposed to be of *honest reputation, and of the best sort as can be got in this kind.* However, some of the ladies were no such thing: they robbed from the dead and the dying, and even resorted to murdering those close to death, by placing a wet cloth over their victim's faces, so that there would be no incriminating signs of a struggle.

When the bodies of victims of the plague had been found, the plague-cart, piled high with corpses, would make its round in the evening to take the dead to the plague-pits. In front of the cart was a *Bell-man*, who would ring his bell and cry, " *Bring out your dead."*

## Abracadabra

People resorted to desperate measures to protect themselves. The rich were advised that they should take three drams of laudanum, while one improbable concoction called for *Four and 20 grams of unicorns horn.* The poor, meanwhile, had to make do with cheaper alternatives, such as smoking tobacco - children were positively encouraged to inhale. One of the most popular methods was to apply an animal to your lower extremities, such as a decapitated pigeon, which would draw out the corrupt substances from your body. Some people even tried to infect themselves with syphilis in the belief that it might offer some protection against plague. The rationale being that you used one poison to drive out another.

Many turned to wearing charms and witchcraft to try to protect themselves:

75

*As if the plague was not the hand of God, but a kind of possession of an evil spirit, and that it was to be kept off with crossings, signs of the zodiac, papers tied up with so many knots, and certain words or figures written on them, as particularly the word Abracadabra, formed in triangle or pyramid,*

## The Flaming Sword

In the year 1598, there was a terrible famine in the city. A desperate mayor even cancelled the toll on corn to try to attract grain into the city, to feed the starving population. To clear the poor from the city, the Assembly issued an order against building cottages; and *sturdy beggars* were put into the stocks.

On the night of 22nd August 1602, *a wonderful exhalation of fiery colour* was seen, *like a canopy over the city.* Astrologers believed that the plague was the result of the malign influence of planets or comets, the flaming swords of God, and were omens of approaching disasters. In September 1602, the great plague began in Chester, which would persist until February 1606. An unspecified number of people died in 1604; 650 in 1603; 986 in 1604; 812 in 1605, and about 100 in 1606. In total, over 2,500 people were taken by the plague.

The plague is said to have started in a house of a *Musissioner* (Musician) named Glover in St. John,s Lane, where seven quickly died of the disease. The Assembly made further restriction against cottages: houses were not to be divided into separate households, and citizens were not to have more than one lodger.

Minutes for September 1602 show that the fair was to be cancelled in view of the outbreak in London, and contributions were to be made to poor families in the city already infected. On the 20th January following it was reported that:

*Diverse lewde and evyll disposed persons for their owne private gaine have carryed diverse clothes, apparrell and other goodes of persons deceased ... of the plague... constables... ymmediately.. shall cuse the wearing apparell and bedddclothes.. to be.. burned.*

However, valuable clothes were to be buried for a season, then washed, scoured and cleaned and reused.

In 1603, many plague victims were quarantined in cabins, called *Pest Houses*, used for the first time in Chester. These were built at the riverside, close to the New Tower (the Water Tower). Most of the victims would never return home. St. Peter's Parish records show:

*xxd (20d) was paid to Bedforde, clerk of St Peter's for making up the accomptees for collections for the cabins which were built at the water side, near the new tower and quarries without the Wall, for the isolation of the infected.*

Burials caused other problems, *paid for v pounds of pitch to perfume the churche after the buryall of Widow Tropp for she died of the sickness viiid (8d).*

## Hot in the City

In 1604, the disease was *very hot* in the city and a great number of people were sent to the cabins. Some of the justices of the peace and a *great number of citizens* fled into the surrounding countryside. However, Edward Dutton, the mayor, bravely stayed in the city, although some of his children and servants died of the plague. The Court of Exchequer was moved to Tarvin, the Michaelmas Assizes were held at Nantwich, all the fairs were cancelled, and the watch was not kept on Midsummer Eve.

People in suburbs contained within city parishes had the major problem of having to bury their dead within the city walls. Whereas, Cestrians wanted to avoid all contact with their infected neighbours. It was agreed that Upton people could bury plague dead at St. Oswald's (then housed in the south transept of Chester Cathedral). However, they were to do it at six o'clock in the evening, to carry white sticks coming and going, and not to converse with any citizen or go into any house. In addition, a brick wall had to be demolished to avoid contact with Cestrians:

*... (coffins) may be carryed into the said Greene church yarde of St. Werburghes (the Cathedral) the usual way of Buryall unto the said church yarde untill they come unto the neerer end of the Bricke Wall adjoyninge to the house of Richard Bavand alderman deceased and by that way to be Carryed into the said Church yard, And thatt yt shall be lawful for the said inhabitants of Upton. During this tyme of Sickness to pull downe a little stonne wall there beinge for the better and redier Conveyinge of the said deade bodyes that way...*

### Carrying white sticks

### Based on C17th woodcut

### Plague stone in Upton

*Photo: Roy Wilding*

A plague stone once stood at the junction of Upton crossroads, opposite the War Memorial (it is now sited in Upton churchyard). This stone was used for the safe purchase of goods: money for goods was put in vinegar, which had been poured into the stone's receptacle, to try to stop the spread of the disease:

*It is true people used all possible precaution. When anyone bought a joint of meat in the market they would not take it off the butcher's hand, but took it off the hooks themselves. On the other hand, the butcher would not touch the money, but have it out into a pot full of vinegar, which he kept for that purpose. The buyer carried always small money to make up any odd sum, that they might take no change.*

## The Golden Talbot

In 1608, plague started in Chester at the Talbot, in Eastgate Street, and 14 people died there. (The hotel was built for the Grosvenors of Eaton, but incorporated some of the fabric of an ancient inn called the White Talbot or Golden Talbot - the Grosvenor crest - and later the Royal Hotel. The old inn was destroyed in the bombardment during the Civil War siege. It is now called the Grosvenor.)

Chester appears to have experienced a severe visitation in 1610. Many in Chester and Liverpool died of plague. In the same year, Ruthin Assembly, North Wales, demanded that anyone who attended their fair must have a certificate stating their good health and that goods must not be brought from infected places.

In 1625, when plague broke out again in Chester, an attempt was made to

78

limit the number of strangers entering Chester, particularly from the south: *The gates of the city were watched night and day for a long time, that no Londoners or wares should enter the city.*

Many who came to the city had to stay in barns and stables for a month, to see if they were clean from infection. Extra precautions were taken at fair time. No fairs were held in Chester in 1631 or 1636, when wares had to be stored outside the city for a month and any porter viewing the goods was not admitted back in the city for a month.

## City of Sorrows

*When sorrows come,*
*they come not [as] single spies,*
*but in battalions.*

Just a few months after the siege of Chester ended a virulent strain of plague started in 1647. The pestilence was so bad that Chester just could not cope, and Parliament issued an 'Ordinance for the Reliefe of Chester':

*Wheras Chester is grievously visited with the pestilence, very few families being clear; by reason whereby almost all persons of ability have left the said city, there remaining for the most part only the poor, who are altogether deprived of trading, and if not presently relieved are likely to perish for want, and endanger infecting the adjacent counties. And whereas the County of Chester is exceedingly impoverished by the late war; tis ordered that the ministers... earnestly move their people to contribute for the relief of the said inhabitants.*

## Dog-Days

*Dog-Days - Period during part of July and August about the time of Heliacal or Cosmical rising of Sirius, the Dog-Star, considered from ancient times the hottest and most unwholesome period of the year.*

During the 23 weeks period from the 22nd June 1647 to the end of November 1647, it was calculated that 2,032 inhabitants of Chester died. A terrible figure, when the total population was probably no greater than 10,000, and many of that number had already fled the city. Not unexpectedly, the disease was at its height from July to August, when the rats and fleas were at their most active.

In the Minute Book of the Company of Barber Chirurgeons (surgeons) of Chester for July 2nd 1647, is the following entry:

79

*Being then the tyme of the Lord's Dreadful visitacon of this Cittie of Chester; fro wch, praysed be God of heaven, who hath in mercy stayed his Judgement, and pmiited a remnant to survive to give him praise this day.*

This was at the beginning of July but, by the end of the year, five of the Company's 24 members were to die.

The long term effects of the plague were so destructive that:

*The city's extinction as a port is generally ascribed to the silting up of the river Dee, but it would seem to be a reasonable supposition that this slaughter of citizens contributed to that extinction. Coming so soon after the prolonged siege of the city, the impact of this bubonic plague must have been a terrible one, it seems probable that the combined effects of siege and the visitation decisively altered the history of Chester, dealing the city a blow from which it never fully recovered.*

## God's Providence

God's Providence House in Watergate Street is known for this inscription '*God's Providence is Mine Inheritance*'. It was built, according to the inscription, in 1652, and it is said that the phrase refers to the house's escape from a visitation of the plague. The story could very possibly be true because:

*They [householders] locked themselves up and kept hid till the plague was over; and many families, foreseeing the approach of the distemper, laid up stores of provisions sufficient for their whole families, and shut themselves up, and that so entirely that they were neither seen or heard of till the infection was quite ceased, and then came abroad sound. Merchants were particularly remarkable, who kept their houses like little garrisons besieged suffering none to go in or out or come near them...*

**God's Providence House
before rebuilding**

Seamen and their families also kept safe, by mooring off land and stocking up with non-perishable provisions like grain for baking bread, cheeses, beer, wines and spirits etc.

In 1654, both Chester and Tarvin were struck by the plague. Judging from a petition that the sheriffs of Chester presented to the Protector on April 28th, the disease must have been an epidemic in Chester by a very mild and early spring of that year, with a *very hot May.* Parliament had ordered that *the sheriffs should keep their courts monthly in the Common Hall of Pleas in Chester Castle,* but the petition prayed that as Chester was plague-stricken and the sickness was spreading, the people could not safely attend a court held in the castle. The assizes were duly held in Nantwich.

## *Intermezzo*

The year 1665 saw the last recorded large-scale outbreak of plague in Chester. In the same year, the Great Plague of London took away 100,000 lives. There is a common misconception that the Fire of London killed off the plague. However, the truth is that the plague died off as a result of the cold weather, improvements in sanitation and building construction, the increased development of immunity and a change in the type of rats. Although the plague subsequently returned, it never visited again on a large scale.

At a seminar at the 1999 British Veterinary Associations annual conference, Vic Simpson, a representative of the governments Veterinary Laboratories Agencies, stated that the bacterium responsible for the Black Death, which ravaged Europe and Asia between the 14th and the 17th centuries, could find its way back to Britain. He said black rats, the bacterium's hosts had recently reappeared in some parts of the UK. Mr Simpson said that the bacterium could find its way back into the UK as a result of international trade. Rats with the disease could get into the UK in sealed containers carried by boats or planes and spread the infection to black rats already in the country. Although the plague is now treatable if caught early, Mr Simpson warned that vigilance was necessary to stop a mass outbreak. A vaccine also exists against plague, but is not effective immediately and not therefore suitable for use in an epidemic.

81

# Ye olde Cathedral City

## *A tale of two cities*

Victorian 'black and white' buildings give a very false image of 'old' Chester. They are elegant pastiches in the Tudor style and very different from the ramshackle originals of early days. Despite their timber appearance, Victorian buildings were generally built in brick. Often only the street elevation was timbered. They were larger, taller and more ornate than the earlier buildings.

Until recent times, buildings had distinct styles and regional differences. Before the canal and the railway age, local materials had to be used for all but the grandest buildings because of the difficulty and cost of transportation. Methods of construction also developed regional variations, depending on local knowledge and expertise. For centuries, timber was the most commonly used building material in the Chester area.

The dense forest of the Cheshire plain provided good cheap building wood for most purposes and ships timbers were also available. Until the beginning of the 18th century, most houses in Chester were timber-framed. Oak was the most popular and durable wood, but uncontrolled felling took its toll. Oak became expensive, so that chestnut, elm and imported softwoods were also used.

## *Rats' nests*

A timber-framed building, as the name implies, is a self-supporting framework of timbers. The spaces between are covered or in-filled to form the walls, roofs and floor. These houses can vary enormously depending on the arrangement of timbers, but the walls always present the appearance of a wooden grid. In larger houses, timbers were added for decoration in a variety of different patterns. The spaces between the exposed timbers were tradition-ally filled with 'wattle and daub' - panels of woven staves, usually of hazel but occasionally of briar, daubed on both sides with clay, dung and straw plaster.

Thatch was once the most common roofing material in the Chester area. Reeds were cheap and plentiful on the banks of the River Dee and from marl pits. Heather, brushwood and straw were also used. However, thatched timber-framed buildings had two great disadvantages: the obvious risk of fire and the unseen but deadly risk of disease, particularly plague. The living conditions of the ordinary Cestrian made bubonic plague principally a disease of the poor. However, it is not a disease associated with dirt and destitution like typhus fever.

The house-rat, which hosts the flea that transmits the plague bacillus, is a natural climber and a good burrower in relatively soft material. It was the 'soft-walled' dwelling house, with its thatched roof, its dark, unventilated, humid interior, and its earthen floor, that the rat and the flea found mutually congenial conditions to multiply. The plague disappeared in Chester about 1666. Numerous theories have been put forward for its departure, including sanitary measures and better control of the rat population. The brick-built houses of the gentry, with their slated or tiled roof were hostile environments to the house-rat, and perhaps the national development of this type of dwelling was the most important single factor in the eventual disappearance of the house-rat: and therefore plague from Britain. In 1670, the City Assembly inadvertently killed two birds with one stone. It is certain that the city authorities had no idea of the role of the house rat in the spread of the plague, but when the Assembly ordered that:

*...for the ornament and security of this Citty from fire...all houses now erected or herafter to bee erected in Foregatestreetre, Eastgatestreete, Northgatestreete and Bridgestreete of this Citty shall be covered with slate or tyle and not thatched.*

This sounded the house-rats' death-knell.

## *Islands in the Sun*

*Bishop Bridgeman cottages of 1642*

*Photo:Mike Penney*

The population density of the Cathedral precinct, which include Abbey Gateway, Abbey Square, Abbey Street and Abbey Green, has always been sparse in comparison with the rest of the city. The Cathedral precinct was isolated from the mass of the population of Chester. It covered a large area of the city, but with only a small population of its own. In 1840 only 329 populated the precinct out of a total Chester population of about 23,000. Excluding the properties of the gentry in other parts of the city, the rest of the citys mass of dwellings were crammed within the city walls or crowded along the riverbank. Chester Cathedral lay clerks were fortunate to live in very early examples of stone dwellings. In 1662, Bishop John Bridgeman had four cottages built on the site of the abbey kitchen. Of the four originally built, only two still exist. They are fine examples of stone buildings dating from this time. The stones used in their construction were almost certainly reused from the demolished abbey buildings.

*Cobbles and wheelers in Abbey Square*
*Photo: Mike Penney*

In the 1750s, the formal Georgian terrace was introduced to Chester, when the cathedral authorities redeveloped an area of the abbey precinct which had contained the monastic brewery, bakehouse and kitchens. The houses on the north and west of Abbey Square, built between 1754 and 1761, followed the pattern of the standard London style Georgian terrace. They are constructed in brick with stone dressings and a parapet above the cornice conceals a low-pitched slate roof. The sash windows are carefully proportioned, with the tallest being on the first floor, lighting the main rooms. The rooms have good light and are well ventilated. In addition they are well proportioned with high ceilings. These are in stark contrast to the dark and cramped dwellings of the poor.

The external area of the Cathedral precinct was cobbled together with flat stones or wheelers, laid almost like the later railways that prevented too much discomfort to the occupants of the rather basically sprung carriages of the 18th century. Unlike most of the rest of Chester's mainly unpaved highways, horse dung and other waste could easily be removed from these surfaces.

## Cool clear water

The Cathedral precincts are on well-drained bedrock at the highest part of the city. The Cathedral may always have had a good supply of pure water. In 1536, Dr Wall the sub-dean, when he was Prior of St Werburgh's, built a conduit to supply his convert with water from the springs in Boughton. In 1600, John Tyrer, a lay clerk in the Cathedral, was licensed by the City Assembly to build a tower above the Bridgegate to supply water from the Dee for the population of Chester.

Chester's water supply was taken principally from the River Dee, into which the contents of the city's sewers flushed. Most complaints about the quality of water occurred after heavy rain stirred up mud from the riverbed. In the early 19th century, private water filters were used only in the richer class of house, including the exclusive properties of Abbey Square. This was life saving, because cholera bacteria can only survive for short periods of time in filtered water.

## Rough and ready

The food of poorer people was unattractive. Bread made from rye or barley was generally eaten with cheese or butter, though white bread made from wheat flour was becoming more popular in Georgian times. Cheap meat was made into broth. Vegetables such as carrots, parsnips and cauliflower were eaten. For the first time tea and sugar became cheap enough for most people to enjoy in small amounts. However, the thirteen inmates of the Hospital of St John the Baptist (where the Bluecoat is sited) did not fare too badly for they were given:

*A good loaf daily, a great dish of pottage, a piece of flesh or fish, and half a gallon of competant ale.*

Preservation of food was limited to salting, drying and pickling. Contamination of all sorts was common. Hygienic storage of food and drink was impossible in the poorer dwellings. The rich ate many different kinds of meat, especially beef and mutton, as well as fish and game. They often drank fine wines, which they preferred served cold (both red and white). The gentry had the advantage of cool cellars or even icehouses where food and drink could be stored in relative safety.

Rough ale was the main tipple of the poor. During the period 1720 to 1750 gin drinking became popular. Gin was very cheap, advertised as drunk for a penny, dead drunk for twopence. It was also dangerous, since it could cause blindness, madness and even death. Many people of all classes were addicted to tobacco or snuff, which was often contaminated with other dreadful substances.

## La Dolce Vita

The rich often dined rather too well. Henry Prescott, who was Deputy Registrar of Chester Diocese, recorded in his diary for the 1st February 1716/17:

*.....go to prayers in the church. After this, Mr Townsend and I go to the Glass-House, where Mr Hulton and the rest of the coursing company. A good dinner of spar-ribb, stewd hoggs puddings & mince pies, well don & eaten with keen appetite. The ale (now good) flows round with the discourse....*

However, it was a very different matter for the poor people, as Prescott's entry in his diary for 15th June 1706/ 07, recording the visit of the Earl of Pembroke to Chester, shows:

*I run in the stream of spectators. The table is loaden with a splendid copia of sweat meats, to which wine is added, the room full, the treat is dispersed in tollerable order, some divercion is made by throwing out some of the sweat meats into the street, where the mobb after scrambling take the sweat meat deep out of the dirt.*

## Quack medicine

Medical knowledge and treatment of disease in Georgian Britain was still primitive. There were no effective treatments for the constantly recurring endemic diseases such as typhoid, measles, influenza or tuberculosis. In addition, epidemics of smallpox or cholera caused devastation. Private physicians, surgeons and apothecaries were numerous. One modern medical historian commented that:

*The low therapeutic efficacy (uselessness) of Georgian medicine (meant that) quack medicine could vie with on regular terms on somewhat approaching parity.*

In other words conventional medicine was not much better than quack medicine, and therefore little reliance could be placed upon the medicines and remedies available at the time. Contemporary newspapers frequently contained advertisements with ridiculous claims for 'wonder' medicines and cures. A leading retailer of 'genuine medicines' in Chester was J Poole, printer and bookseller of Eastgate Street. His claims included:

*A balsam of liquorice root "endued with the most powerful pectoral, healing and deterging qualities"; Hill's genuine Ormskirk medicine, "which infallibly cures the Bite of a Mad Dog"; Dr Greenough's tincture for preserving teeth; and oriental vegetable cordial, for bowel disorders.*

One of Henry Prescott's recommended remedies was snail water: *Water in which snails had been cooked.* Prescott regarded it as one of his more successful remedies for pain and insomnia, referring to it on several occasions as an *opiate.*

## John Haygarth

During the Georgian Period the population of Britain more than doubled. This was partly because people married earlier and had more children, and partly because doctors were beginning to understand the human body and to learn more about how to treat some diseases.

In 1796 Dr Edward Jenner discovered that milkmaids who caught cowpox never caught smallpox, a disease that killed many children and scarred thousands of others. He 'vaccinated' people with a mild dose of cowpox, which protected them from the killer disease. Over 150 new hospitals were built in Britain.

Some, like Guy's and St George's in London, were used for training doctors and midwives. However, operations were still dangerous. Surgeons worked fast because there were no effective anaesthetics. Most of their patients died in agony of shock, or through infection because there were no antiseptics. The slightest cut or bruise could be fatal, resulting in blood poisoning and 'lockjaw' (from tetanus).

The most important medical foundation in 18th century Chester was the General Infirmary.

In 1755, the infirmary opened in the upper part of the Blue Coat Hospital. The first patient was a William Thompson of St Mary's Parish, being admitted with a wounded hand in November 1755. Ailments treated during the first year included asthma, consumption, epilepsy, dropsy, hysterics, jaundice, leprosy, rheumatism, scrofula,scurvy, ulcerated legs and worms.

The temporary accommodation soon became inadequate and, in 1761, a new building was opened in St Martin' s-in-the-Fields, with beds for 100 patients. Sick from Chester, Cheshire and North Wales could be admitted upon recommendation of subscribers to the infirmary. The nurses, whose status in the medical world was very low at this time, were encouraged:
*To obey the matron as their mistress and to behave with tenderness to the patients and with civility and respect to strangers.*

In 1767, Dr John Haygarth (1740-1827) was appointed as physician to the infirmary. In 1784, he was responsible for converting an attic storey for the reception and isolation of fever patients. This was the first fever ward in the country. In 1790, a sedan chair was purchased to carry fever patients into the infirmary. Other examples of his innovation were the installation of hot baths and the introduction of remedial treatment by salt-water bathing.

Haygarth' s special interests were the prevention of smallpox and the treatment of fever patients. In 1774, he conducted a population census of Chester, which included questions about typhus fever and smallpox. In his paper 'Observations on the population and Diseases of Chester in 1774', he advocated the removal of fever patients to separate fever wards. He found that out of a population of just over 14,000, only 1,060 had never contacted smallpox.

Largely owing to Haygarth, a Smallpox Society was formed in 1778, with the aim of promoting inoculation and preventing the casual smallpox in Chester (almost 20 years before Jenner). This was so successful that, by 1782, the number of deaths from casual smallpox had been reduced by almost half. Leeds and Liverpool were to follow Chester's example.

## *Squalor*

In the 18th century, scientific medicine was still at a fetal stage and life expectancy was generally short. The likelihood of longevity together with a pleasant existence was probably linked to status and wealth. However, over-indulgence by the rich was certainly a negative factor.

Some of Chester's population had outside lavatories, at a convenient distance, with a hole underneath where the contents could be covered over with a layer of earth or ashes. This earth closet was housed in a little outbuilding known as the privy. That is why the back yard was so important. Other kinds of household waste were also deposited in the back yard, not only organic material such as peelings and pan-scrapings, but also the ashes and cinders from the fire. For this purpose a pit or enclosure of some kind was made, called an ashpit, middenstead, or boghole. The most convenient place for this midden was next to the privy, so that ashes for throwing into it were close at hand. Many properties had no yards at all.

Dwellings built in courts and blind-alleys had outside space only at the front, and usually very little of it. Even where there were yards, many completely lacked any kind of structural privy or midden and the inhabitants relieved themselves at random in the surroundings.

The 'privey-midden system' was all very well for scattered farmhouses and cottages in the countryside, but in a city like Chester, ever more tightly crammed with people and dwellings, it was a different matter altogether. The problem was how to get rid of all this stinking rubbish and filth. In the absence of sewers there were two ways of getting rid of liquid waste. Some houses, or groups of houses and courtyard dwellings, had a deep pit (perhaps covered over), into which liquid could drain through pipes. The idea was that water would naturally seep away through the sides and bottom, leaving only solid matter in the pit. (The liquid waste that drained from the pit would, of course, eventually pollute any drinking water in the vicinity) This was called a cesspit. The other way was to tip the waste into the street and leave it to find its own way.

Not only was every family home intimately affected by the homes of neighbouring families, it was also dependent on neighbours for vital supplies amid the utmost poverty and filth. Meat, milk and bread were provided by methods, which relied very heavily on other people in the immediate neighbourhood. Often, bakehouses were located in cellars, and the ovens for baking were underground. Many small slaughterhouses and dairies were dotted throughout the city, in close proximity to human dwellings and cesspits.

## Autumn leaves

During the end of September and early October, influenced by approaching cold, flies began to gather in the houses for the winter. This was the dangerous period, associated with the *close of the summer, the fall of the leaf, and the invasion of the common housefly.*

The connection between diarrhoeal sickness and the immediate environment of Chester's warren of tightly packed dwellings lay in the life-cycle and feeding habits of the house fly. The housefly breeds in rubbish, stable manure, and decaying matter generally. The principal breeding places were the middens connected with stables situated in the midst or on the edges of the city. Most of the middens probably belonged to the people who had only one horse or donkey. They made a living by carting or coal dealing and, in addition, middens were a valuable source of revenue for their manure.

As an example, the census return of 1851 records that a cow-keeper lived in Shipgate Street, which is just within the City Walls. Even as late as 1929, my own family kept cab horses well within the City Walls, at the Skeleton Yard behind King's Buildings. It was called the Skeleton Yard because it used to be a veterinary surgery (Horse Hospital) and there was a full skeleton of a horse hanging over the yard entrance: *whose bleached bones glowed eerily in the silvery moonlight.*

**Cow-keeper in Shipgate Street**
*Engraving courtesy of David Cummings*

In summary, it is almost certain that life for the fortunate people who lived in the cathedral precinct was heaven compared to the lot of the poor ordinary Cestrian.

90

*Skeleton Yard*
*Old Photo courtesy of Len Morgan*

# Chester Cathedral Early Days

## *The men in black*

The first personnel of Chester Cathedral were drawn from pre-Reformation clerics. The last abbot of St Werburgh's Abbey, Thomas Clark, became the first dean of the building's new use as the Cathedral Church of Christ and the Blessed Virgin Mary. However, he died after only a few months in the job. In October 1541, Henry Mann became the next Dean of Chester. Born in Lancashire about 1500, he became a Carthusian monk in 1521. He rose to be Prior of the Monastery of Sheen in 1535. In 1539, he surrendered his monastery into the king' s hands and received the (then) enormous pension of £166 13s 4d.

The first sub-dean was Dr William Wall, ex-Warden of Grey Friars in Chester, whose house had been confiscated in the Dissolution of 1538. He is famous for laying conduit (1536) to supply water from Boughton springs. He died in 1574 and had the distinction of burial under the west window of the Cathedral.

The senior prebendary was Nicholas Bucksey, who had been Prior of St

Werburgh's. He became treasurer of the Cathedral, a proctor in the Convocation and, later on, Arch-Deacon of Chester. Thus the first three members of the new Cathedral body were all either ex-monks or ex-friars: Mann the Carthusian, Wall the Franciscan and Bucksey the Benedictine.

Whatever their religious beliefs, it appeared that:

*Whatsoever king might reign, they would keep their stalls in Chester Cathedral, for they managed to conform to the regimes of Henry VIII, Edward VI, Mary and Elizabeth.*

Little is known of the remaining four prebendaries: Thomas Newton, John Hunt, Thomas Radford and Roger Smith. However, they all died at the end of 1543 or the beginning of 1544, perhaps from an outbreak of plague. Next to the prebendaries came six minor canons, called petycanons. Whereas the prebendaries were called Mr, the minor canons were always called Sir, which appears to be the inferior title in those days.

The choir was composed of six lay clerks or conducts and eight choristers. One of the lay clerks seems to have been a priest, for he appears as "Vyker of St Oswald's" in a Survey of 1540 and drew a pension from the Abbey of 33/4. The deacon and sub-deacon, called gospellor and epistoler, were also called Sir, though they would probably be only in minor orders as their title implies. The organist was John Bircheleye, formerly schoolmaster at the monastery. He too had a pension of £6.

From time to time human problems arose within the Cathedral, and the dean and chapter were forced to take disciplinary action in the following three cases:

*In 1709, the organist and choirmaster was expelled for fathering a bastard. The conducts and vergers were warned against absence from services and excessive drinking in 1727, and in 1746 a prebendary was deprived for immorality.*

## Flunkies

According to the Statutes of the Cathedral, the domestic staff of the Cathedral was to consist of two vergers, two porters (one of whom was to be a barber) one butler and two cooks. However, the accounts show that in 1541, three years before the Statutes were issued, there were three butlers, one for the dean, one for the canons, and one for the petycanons. In addition, there was no fewer than five cooks, one for the Dean and two each for the other two bodies. There was also a baker (Robert ap Willy'am) and a water carrier:

*(Dec 24, 1541) to Hughe Hey watttercarior for s'ving the Deane and Canons of water .. IOs.*
*(March 31, 1542) to the Smythe for shoeing the water horse this dim. yer past 55 4d.*

One of the porters was Edward ap Gryffyn who kept the gate of the monastery and was still employed there during the intervals between reigns. The petycanons' cook was another link with the abbey, for he was Thomas Goose or Gose, formerly servant of Abbot Clarke and tenant of *Cellarer's Meadow with all the tithe of hay and corn in the Bache.*

In addition, there were six bedesmen who were to be nominated by the Crown and assist the vergers in the Cathedral:
*They must be poor and indigent persons, or who have been disabled or mutilated in battle, or otherwise disabled and reduced to poverty and wretchedness. They were called almsmen or King's almsmen, and they received £6 13s 4d a year.*

In 1541, the 'King's School or Free School' was founded by Henry VIII. From the early 17th century until 1876 it was housed in the Cathedral refectory. The original foundation of the school provided for a master and an usher who were to:
> *teach Latin to 24 poor and friendless boys....of good capacity (so far as is possible) and capable of learning.*

Fee-paying pupils were taken as well as the foundation scholars.

The Cathedral community appears to have been insular, ultra-conservative and have a rigid social structure; its effects on Cathedral burials is analyzed in the next section.

## Number of burials

There were 442 burials recorded in the Cathedral Registers for the years 1687 to 1812 (excluding the period covered by the missing registers for 1718 to 1735).

Over this 108-year period, there were 229 female and 213 male burials. The arithmetic mean or average was just over four burials per annum. In fact, during these years, burials per annum for males or females never reached double figures. The maximum number of female burials was nine per annum

93

and for males was six per annum. The mode for female burials was one per annum on 36 occasions and for male burials was one per annum on 35 occasions.

It may seem remarkable, in an age with such high mortality rates, that there are no records for female burials on 11 (yearly) occasions or male burials on 19 occasions. There is no evidence to suggest that the registers are inaccurate. However, it is difficult to believe that, on so many occasions, there were no deaths. This might mean that burial in the Cathedral was "exclusive" and restricted to a "chosen" few.

## Seasonal variations

In order to identify any seasonal variation in the death rate, the cumulative burial rate per month was plotted for the 108 year period already specified between 1687 to 1812, less the years between 1718 to 1735 inclusive.

From the calculations it is clear that there is a definite seasonal variation in burials per month. The least number of burials occurred in September, rising in the autumn and early winter to a high level in December. A high level of burials continued throughout the winter months, even through the spring until May. Not unexpectedly, there were far fewer burials in summer then in winter.

## Composition of burials

Although full background details of the deceased are not always included in the registers, at least 37% of Cathedral burials were composed of clerics, associated personnel and their families. The remaining 63% were composed of lay males and females. However, a proportion of these may also have had cathedral associations that are not stated in the registers.

## Tinker Tailor

It may be reasonable to assume that Cathedral burials were restricted to only rich and important people. However, reference to the burial registers shows this assumption to be absolutely wrong. The criteria for cathedral burial appear to include the following: association with the clergy, residence within the Cathedral precincts and/or attendance at the Cathedral, and wealth or social status.

At least 37% of burials were composed of clerics, associated personnel and their families. Burials ranged from the bishop to the bishop's cook and from the Chancellor of Chester's wife to a verger's daughter. Included were people

94

associated with the 'Free School'. The privilege of Cathedral burial also extended to the families of deceased clergy and associated personnel: The widow of a conduct (chorister) and the mother of the Head of the Free School.

About 63% of burials were composed of lay males and females. As previously stated, some of these may also have had clerical associations which are not stated in the registers. Sadly, in many cases, the registers tell us very little about those that are buried. However, in a large number of instances, there is a good deal of data available. There are people included such as: the late Governor of New York State, attorneys, military officers, aldermen, son of a sea captain, and dancing master. Also included are: a "Brasier", publicans, a mason and a gardener. The latter two may have been Cathedral staff, but this is not stated in the registers. There were a small number of paupers buried in the Cathedral, but these included elderly ladies, who may have been widows or daughters of deceased clergy or their helpers.

## *Burial locations*

In a small number of cases the actual place of burial is specified in the registers: the choir of the Cathedral, the south cloister, the maiden aisle and the Broad "Isle" (the nave). However, the sample size is, perhaps, too small to draw any firm conclusions, regarding the link between burial location and social status. However, it may not be unreasonable to assume that there were certain prestigious burial locations within the Cathedral, such as the west window, ie. William Wall, was buried in 1574, "Under the West Window of the Cathedral".

In 1693, a Captain Seth Mort was entered in the cathedral burial register, but was buried in the "Parish Church". This Parish Church may have been St Oswald's Church, which was located in the south transept of the cathedral, which was also called the 'Merchant Aisle'. Care has to be taken to conclude that the transept was always St Oswald''s Church in the strict sense of the word. The power of holding service during the intervals of cathedral service was the limit of the right of the parishioners. It is recorded, that in 1672, John Deane, butcher, sexton of the parish of St Oswald's:
*Begged pardon on his bended knees of the dean and chapter for having broken ground for a grave in the Church of St Werburgh, otherwise sometime called by the name of St Oswald.*

On December 3rd 1708, there was a note of a petition of the parishioners of St Oswald's to the dean and chapter for a gallery, which was not granted until September 6th of the following year.

## Buried in wool

In the case of Thomas Scofield, Attorney, who died in 1689, we are told that he was buried in wool:
*The Ceste for bur: in Woolen is kept in St. Marie's Church.*

The "Burial in Wool Acts, 1667 and 1678", were intended to support the wool trade. The Acts enacted that corpses should be buried in wool. The 1678 Act stated that:
*No corpse of any person (except those who shall die of the plague), shall be buried in any shirt, shist, sheet or shroud or anything whatsoever, made or mingled with flax, hemp, silk, hair, gold or silver, or in any stuff or thing other than what is made of sheep's wool only...*

A relative of the deceased was required, according to the Act, to swear an affidavit (recorded in the registers), within eight days of the event that a "woollen burial" had taken place or else a fine of £5 was levied not only on the estate of the deceased, but on anyone connected with the burial. However, the only "woollen" burial recorded was for the Attorney Scofield.

Apart from this isolated case, Chester Cathedral does not appear to have complied with (some or all parts of) the Act. In addition, it is recorded that, also in 1669, Jeoffrey Malborn was buried in *"Linnen"* in the Broad Isle. According to the 'Local Historian Encyclopedia', "These Acts were repealed in 1814 but they had by then fallen into disuse".

## Stamp Act 1783

From 1784 to 1794, entry was made of the duty paid on the burials. A duty of 3d was imposed on each parish register. The incumbent was given a 10% commission for collection

## Shifting sands

Structural changes to the Cathedral, relaying the floor and inter-cutting of the graves, has made identification of the majority of burials impossible. The only constant factor in the history of the Cathedral structure is change. In 1557, a Visitation recorded that:
*The Church wants repair, the Church yard is defiled by animals & cattle...*
and that *Thomas Green rents the Church yard.*

In 1559, it was ordered that the *"Shrines"* be destroyed. During the rest of the 16th century, the Cathedral appears to have been in a bad state of repair. In

1600, the Nave floor was paved in stone for the first time:
*The flagging of the long West Ile (Nave) of the Minister was this year (1600) begun by Dean Nutter.*

A few years before, it was said to be lying unpaved like a barn floor. The work was carried out by the Cathedral lay clerk John Tyrer (who also carried out the works for the later water tower above the Bridgegate). It is recorded that earth was carted from the church. Although restoration work took place in 1607-1610, the Cathedral was later occupied and damaged by Parliamentary troops during the Civil War.

The 18th century was kinder to the Cathedral. In 1702, there was a collection in Cheshire churches for its restoration. The Cathedral registers state that: *This year (1749) the Cathedral cleaned, painted and beautified...* Also that... *This year (1751) the Choir layd with marble & the cloyster covered with a new roof by William Stradford, LLD Comissary of Richmond.*

In 1777, the Nave was again repaved, after 177 years of wear.

The 19th century restorations transformed the Cathedral into the familiar structure we know today. Restorations took place in 1818 and 1843, by Harrison and Hussey. Gas lighting was installed in 1819. The years 1868-76, saw the major restoration by Sir George Gilbert Scott. Between 1882-87, Sir Arthur Blomfield carried out restoration. In 1889, St Werburgh's Shrine was moved to the Lady Chapel. In the 1880s, the north wall of the north aisle of the Nave was decorated with mosaics designed by J R Clayton. In order to make space for the mosaics, wall monuments or murals had to be removed. Murals to the Potts and Wrench families were re-sited on the south wall of the south aisle of the Nave. The north wall of the Nave has a greater surface area than the south one. Therefore, it may not have been possible to accommodate all the north wall murals on the south wall.

Changes continued into the 20th century, when restoration work was carried out by Giles Gilbert Scott between 1911-13. In 1996, Chester Archaeology excavated parts of the Nave floor. The floor, which was badly worn and dangerous, has recently been completely relayed and under-floor heating installed.

## *Out-of-parish entries*

Out of a total (burial) population of 442, at least 37 were of people from outside the cathedral precincts, which were fairly evenly distributed over the period under examination. At least 14 of the 37 were clergy, or had links with the clergy. A good proportion of the remaining appears to be of the gentry or merchant classes.

There are two particularly interesting entries: George Clark, late Governor of New York and Lucy Jodrell. After returning finally to England, Lieutenant-Governor Clark took up his residence at Hyde, but later moved to Chester, where he died at his house in White Friars in 1760, and was buried in the Cathedral. On the south wall of the nave, under the window nearest the south transept, is a monument to his memory.

Lucy Jodrell was first buried at St Michael's on June 19th 1786, but her body was "removed" to the Cathedral on 3rd February 1808. Sarah Jodrell, a spinster age 89, was also buried in the cathedral on the same date. Their monument is on the south wall of the nave next to the southwest door.

## Age and cause of death

Between 1770 to 1780 and 1808 to 1812, the age of the deceased was recorded. In many cases, the presumed cause of death was also stated. The entries, for this period at least, indicates a mainly elderly male and female population.

References such as *"the good old lady Donnolan"* in 1692 and *"old Mrs Whittingham"* in 1691, appears to reinforce the theory that some, at least, were surviving into old age. Although George Clark's (late Governor of New York) age is not recorded in the registers (1760), we know that he lived well into his 80s. Another example of longevity is Laurence Fogg, who was dean for 26 years (1692-1718) until the age of 88.

From the list below, it can be seen that the stated cause of death in 12 out of 31 cases was through decay or decline. Perhaps decline meant - old age.

Stated Cause of Death:
3 Dropsie, 12 Decay/Decline, 3 Consumption, 3 Cancer, 2 Palsey, 1 Smallpox, 3 Gout, 1 Childbed, 1 Asthma, 1 Lingering Disease, 1 Died Suddenly

## Image and Reality

So the popular image of ye olde Chester is a myth. The image usually peddled is the sanitized version of reality that embraces attractive buildings and quaint customs, important people and momentous events. The reality for most Cestrians, certainly the poorer ones, was of a short and brutal life lived in pain, poverty and filth.

# Odds and Ends

## A Case of Suspended Animation

The following obituary notice appeared in the *Gentleman's Magazine* for April 1801:

*Lately at Chester, aged ninety-two, Christopher Lowe, many years bill-distributor for the Theatre Royal of Chester. This venerable patriarch was a native of Preston, and, when in his 16th year, was afflicted with a fever, of which he apparently died. He was laid out, shrouded and coffined; and nearly three days after his supposed demise, while being carried by four mens shoulders to the grave, he suddenly knocked on the lid of the coffin; and to the ineffable amazement of the carriers and attendants, on opening it, they found honest Christopher in a complete state of resuscitation.*

For many years after, he used to amuse and astonish his neighbours and friends with the *wonderful things he saw in his trance.*

## Murder on the Roodee

At a Coroner's Inquest held in the Common Hall at Chester, on the 1st February 1553, Robert Whalley, merchant, and several other witnesses gave the following evidence against Richard Lewes into the Murder of Richard Gerrat:

*... who on their oath say that Richard Lewes, of Chester, Hammerer, on the 4th December, 5th Edward VI (1553), in the county of the same city, in a certain place called le Rode Dee, under the Walls of the said city, with a sword and shield made attack upon one Richard Gerrat, of the city of Chester, mariner: and with a certain sword of the value of twenty pence, which he had in his hands, struck him upon the head, and gave him a mortal blow; of which blow the said Richard Gerrat languished until the 18th December then next following, on which day he, from the same blow, died. And so the said Richard Lewes did aforesaid Richard Gerrat feloniously kill and murder. And that the said Richard Lewes did, immediately after the said felony, make flight.*

Richard Lewes made his escape and was never heard of again!

## The Coffin in the Wall (see rear cover)

Placed high in a recess in St John's Church Norman ruins is a solid oak coffin with the inscription *Dust to Dust*. There have been many theories and stories told about the origin of this strange coffin and its placement in such a peculiar position. One story goes that it was the coffin of a monk who had murdered one of his brethren at St John's, and at his own death was refused an ordinary Christian burial, either within the church or the churchyard. Another story tells that a dignitary of the church was at his own request buried up there in a standing position, so that, when the last trumpet sounded, he might be ready at once to answer the call.

Yet another story is that a wicked old parishioner was unable to rest in his grave. Old Nick (Satan) heard about this, and helped to place him in the lofty position the coffin now occupies; so that the sinner might look down, in perpetual penance, on the fair world he had defiled by his sins. However, according to an article published in the November 1878 edition of the *Cheshire Sheaf* the real story goes as follows:

*Forty years ago (about 1838), when I was a boy at school, I remember old John Carter, the then sexton of the Cathedral, going with me at my request into St John's Ruins (at that time enveloped within a brick wall, and a portion of the grounds of the old Priory House), to show me the relic and its then fresh-looking inscription.*

*He assured me on the spot that his father, who was sexton of St John's for a great number of years, had in his younger days come upon the coffin while digging in a grave in a long disused part of the churchyard; and had, by the Rector's (Mr. Richardson's) orders, stuck it up in the recess where it still stands, so that it might be out of the way of passers by!*

In Gordon Emery's recent book *Curious Chester*, Gordon describes another story to add to the mystery:

*The unusual coffin in the walls of the ruins is said to have been set up by the Rev. Richardson in 1813. It had been brought by canal boat from Nantwich by the Rev Massey.*

We may never know the true origin of the coffin, but it is clear that a matter of fact incident has given rise in superstitious minds to no end of mystery.
The date of the coffin is probably of the latter half of the 15th century: and the relic has this one element of real interest in it, that it is composed of a single block of oak, which has been hollowed out to receive the body.

## A Deadly Duel

On Tuesday 26th September 1727, Thomas Robinson, gentleman, of Dublin, together with Robert Meredith, gentleman, and others arrived in Chester from Dublin. In the evening of the same day, Robinson, Meredith and the rest of the company who had travelled from Ireland, went to sup together at the Golden Talbot Inn in Eastgate Street. After supper the party continued drinking there until about two or three oclock next morning; in which time some words *happened between Thomas Robinson and Robert Meredith occasioned by Thomas Robinson.*

Robinson then assaulted Meredith by head butting him in the chest, grabbed hold of him and challenged him to a fight. Still holding Meredith, Robinson gave him a sword, held him by the arm and forced him to go to Foregate Street to fight a duel. Robinson and Meredith drew their swords, and Robinson made *several passes* at Meredith and wounded him in several places.

As the duel continued, John Carrick, gentleman, tried to beat the duellists swords down with his own sword to stop the fight and to prevent further injury. Carrick *struck upon the swords of Meredith and Robinson,* but instantly Meredith, in his own defence, gave Thomas Robinson a *mortal wound with the sword.* Meredith held his sword in his right hand and cut Robinson in the left side of the throat:

*From which wound he languished till about eleven of the clock in the last night (the inquest was held on Thursday 28th September 1727), and then dyed of the same wound in the said City.*

The inquest jury found that Robert Meredith did wound and kill Thomas Robinson, in addition, for the record, the jury said that the sword that killed Robinson was valued at one shilling and was now in the custody of the Clerk of the Peace of the City of Chester. It does not appear that Meredith was punished in any way for the slaying of Robinson and the evidence given suggests that he acted in self-defence.

## Terror at the Puppet Show

On the 5th November 1772, ironically on Guy Fawkes Night, one of the worst disasters in the history of Chester occurred at a puppet-show held in Eaton's Room, next door but three from Bishop Lloyd's House in Watergate Street. The Chester Courant of November 10th 1772, ran the following story:

*On Nov. the 5th, a few minutes before nine o'clock in the evening, the inhabitants of this city were greatly alarmed by a loud unusual noise, attended with a shaking of the ground, which everyone imagined to proceed from an earthquake. But the news soon arrived that a large number of people, assembled at a puppet-show, had been blown up by gunpowder, placed in a grocer's warehouse, which was under the room.*

*Amidst the universal consternation and confusion, occasioned by this dreadful calamity, it happened most fortunately that some gentlemen had repaired to the melancholy scene a few minutes after the accident; who gave particular directions that every person who shewed the least signs of life should be immediately carried to the Infirmary, where the physicians and surgeons would be ready to administer every possible means of relief.*

*The number admitted that night was 33, and 20 since, in all 53. Besides 23 dead, and these 53 hospital patients, there appear to be about 30 more in the town who have received some degree of injury, in the shape of slight contusions and burns, - in all about 106.*

The records of the *Inquisition* into the accident held on the 7th November 1772, listed the names of the dead bodies found in the ruins as:

*Elizabeth Hale, Elizabeth French, Anne Peers, George Williams, Elizabeth Williams, Kendrick Eaton, Elizabeth Cook, John Merrijohn, Edward Powell, James Harrison, Elizabeth Allen, John Lawrenson, Timothy Garner, John Hewitt, Mary Ankers, Esther Jones, William Roberts, Elizabeth Williams, and Robert Williams.*

Beneath Eaton's Room was a vault used as the warehouse of a city grocer, including about a third of a ton of gunpowder. At the height of the performance, the store of gunpowder mysteriously ignited wrecking the first storey above. The explosion brought down the floor and the injured and dying spectators into the cellar. Rescuers were at first afraid to enter the ruins for fear of a further explosion or collapse of the building; but a certain Joseph Hand, hearing the groans and the screams of the mutilated and wounded, shouted, *"What is my life more than that of another man?"* and leaped into the ruins, soon to be joined by other helpers! Thirteen city constables were drafted in to keep order amid the mounting hysteria as the labourers searched the wreck.

Funeral sermons were preached in all the city's churches; the bells were tolled, and Chester was a place of grief and mourning. The loss of his son and daughter were too much for one of the city merchants, who never recovered

102

his sanity. The owner of the cellar fell into a fever caused by the shock, and died within a few days. The enormous sum of £630 was collected in the city for the injured and the relatives of the dead.

When Mr Thomas Townshend of the Abbey Square was given the news, he inquired, *"Was anyone of consequence injured?"* and was thereafter known as *Mister Consequence* for his apparent callousness. A Quaker called Thomas Brackenbury, seeing the accident as a divine warning against puppet-shows, published a pamphlet called '*The Explosion: or an Alarming Providential Check to Mortality'.*

The show had been crowded with children, but the scholars and master from a small school in Mainwaring House across the street had a very lucky escape when the master took ill before the show, so that they did not go to the show on that fatal night.

The passage by Eaton's Room, leading back to Commonhall Street, was called Puppet Show Entry. Today this whole area has been replaced with a modern block of property in which a Row level has been retained, and there is no longer any trace of Puppet Show Entry, Eaton's Room or of the tragedy that occurred there on 5th November 1772.

## A Cutting Wind

Returning home late one night, in the early 1980s, to his home in Queen's Park, Dr Philip Higson, lecturer in renaissance history at University College, Chester, experienced something so unpleasant that it still unsettles him to recall it, even after so many years:

*Cutting through on the walk between the [Grosvenor] park railings and the ruins of St John's [Church], to get to the suspension bridge, when he became aware of something rushing towards him along the pathway. First thinking it may be some fool on a bicycle, he reacted by trying to step to one side, but there was a very disturbed whirling in the air. He was too late to get out of the way, thus the entity struck him, but to his amazement, passed right through him! He momentarily felt a snap of cold breath and something unpleasantly malevolent.*

# The Cruel Sea

## Above us the Waves

Chester was the major port of the Northwest since as far back as Roman times. For most of its history, the Port of Chester also included the lower reaches of the River Dee, the estuary and a section of the coast of North Wales. It therefore comes of little surprise that there are many tales of shipwrecks, drowning, press gangs and even pirates. The earliest report of a shipwreck was recorded on a Roman gravestone, found in Chester City Walls north wall (west) in 1891, with the following inscription on it:

*An optio entitled to become a centurion, serving in the century of lucilius Ingenuus, who died by shipwreck. He is buried [here] (possibly the word here was omitted until the body was rescued from the sea, but was never added).*

**Tombstone of a shipwrecked 'optio' at Grosvenor Museum**

Another early story relates to Domyngo de Sasarendo and Fernado de Vitaer, two Spanish sailors, who were drowned between Blacon Head and Burton Head in 1540: *by the fierce flow of water.*

Tobacco has claimed millions of lives through the centuries but in the mid-seventeenth century it claimed a life even before it was smoked when, in dark and stormy weather during 1658, Robert Carr fell from a boat and was drowned when bringing tobacco from Dawpool to Chester.

The Dutch East India Company built the first British yacht. *Mary* which was purchased by the City of Amsterdam, fitted out and presented to King Charles II when he was restored to the English throne in 1660. Officials used luxurious vessels like *Mary*, with grand insignia and decoration on their counters, for tours of duty. Yachts were built for speed (the Dutch word for yacht comes from jagen meaning to hurry or chase) and had large sail areas but shallow draughts. Samuel Pepys sailed in her and noted:

*One of the finest things that I ever saw for neatness and room in so small a vessel.*

King Charles enjoyed sailing against his brother, but wanted an even faster vessel. The following year the *Katherine* was built for him, and the *Mary* was demoted to general service, transporting officials between Dublin and Holyhead, the Irish Sea being described as: *short and broken that Holland built ships are found fittest for that purpose.*

On 25th March 1675, the *Mary* was en route from Dublin to Chester with a crew of 28, plus three noblemen and 43 other passengers. In thick fog, while passing Anglesey in the early hours, she struck the southwest corner of the Skerries (near the site of the lighthouse built thirty-nine years later). Fortunately, she caught in a gully with her long mast touching the rocks. About half those on board were able to scramble ashore where they spent a miserable couple of days before they were rescued. The wreck quickly broke up so that artifacts, guns and masses of iron shot went to the bottom. Of the 74 people on board, 39 survived.

Divers still visit the wreck and Merseyside Museum have over 1,500 objects from the shipwreck. These include many items belonging to her noble passengers, such as silver cutlery, and gold and diamond jewellery.

In 1704, Richard Simmond, owner of the ship *Samuel* of Dublin, was drowned with the master of the ship, when it struck a sandbank on its way to Parkgate. In 1736, Charles Steard, mariner, was flung overboard by the boom of the sloop *The Sea Horse* of Chester and was drowned.

The *Royal Charter*, built by George Cramm at his Sandycroft boatyard, seemed to be jinxed from the very beginning. The first attempt to launch her in 1855 was unsuccessful, despite the use of the side-launching technique developed at Birkenhead. She was eventually driven aground off Moelfre, Anglesey, in October 1859, on a return voyage from Australia with the loss of 400 lives and £300,000 in gold bullion.

These are just a few of the drowning and shipwrecks that occurred in the Port of Chester, many more incidents are recorded in *The Coroners' Reports,* held at Cheshire and Chester Archives.

## The King's Shilling

Although Chester was not a naval base, the press gangs came here searching for able men they could press or force to serve in the fleet. The letter book of Daniel Peck, a Chester merchant, describes his attempts to protect his crews from the menace of the press gang in the early part of the 18th century. In 1798, Peter Martin was executed for shooting at the press gang.

There was another affray in 1808, when a press gang tried to Capture Daniel Jackson, a member of the Chester Volunteers. Daniel had been to sea and, as an able seaman was a prime target for the gangs. However, Jackson's fellow volunteers attempted a rescue, and he was put in the Northgate Gaol for his own protection:

*By this act (putting Jackson in the Northgate Gaol) the volunteers were still more violently incensed, and collecting together in great numbers... they surrounded the prison, which they burst open, and liberated their companion...*

The Mayor's porter, William Dennis, was sacked for being drunk during the affray. However, he was later given his job back, because he had been: *Instrumental in protecting the Press Gang from the fury of the mob...*

## Buccaneers

*Buccaneer: Sea rover, pirate, and unscrupulous adventurer. From the French boucanier, which is derived from boucaner to cure meat on a boucan (i.e. barbecue), a Brazilian word.*

In 1562, the captain of the *James* complained that his ship had been raided by Breton pirates whilst on a voyage to Chester. In 1565, William Birt, of the Forest of Dean, led six men on a raid against a foreign ship moored in the Port of Chester, believing it was Spanish. In the struggle, one of the crew was killed and flung overboard. Only too late, the raiders realised that they had made a big mistake, and that the ship was in fact French! To add to their woes, the cargo was mostly English. They all finished up in the Northgate Gaol.

## The White Ship

Four centuries earlier, according to the chronicler William of Malmesbury:

*No ship ever brought so much misery to England. None was ever so notorious in the history of the world.*

On 25th November, 1120, the White Ship (to give it its French name *Blanche Nef)* sailed from Barfleur, near Cherbourg in France, as part of the royal flotilla of King Henry I of England. On board the White Ship were the cream of Norman society, including Richard, Earl of Chester (1101-1120), and the only two legitimate sons of King Henry I (1070  1135), William and Richard:

*He (Richard, Earl of Chester) married Maude, daughter of Stephen Earl of Bloys ... and had no sooner tasted the pleasures of the marriage bed, but he and the young countess were by the churlish waves, not only prohibited their mutual love embraces, and hopes of future posterity to succeed them, but were deprived of their lives also, as they were sailing for England from France ... he (Richard, Earl of Chester) was about the age of twenty-five years when he was drowned.*

*A merchant ship in the 12th century*

*The master of the ship was Thomas the son of Stephen, who came to King Henry the First, then in Normandy, and ready to take shipping for England, and offered him a mark of gold desiring, that as Stephen his father had transported the Conqueror when he fought against King Harold in England, and was his constant mariner in all his passages between England and Normandy, so that he himself likewise might now have transportation of King Henry with his attendance, as if were in fee; for he had a very good ship called 'Candida Navis', or 'The White Ship'.*

*The king thanked him, but withal told him, he had already made choice of another ship, which he would not change; yet he would commend his two sons, William and Richard, with many others of his nobility; whereat the mariners much rejoiced, and desired the prince to bestow some wine upon them to drink. He gave them three hogshead of wine, wherewith they made themselves sufficiently drunk.*

*There were almost three hundred in this unfortunate ship; for there were fifty skilful oars or galleymen, had they not been intoxicated with wine, which belonged to the ship, besides the young gallants which were to be transported: but now being neither able to govern themselves nor the ship, they suffered it to be split on a rock, and so were all drowned, except one Berolde, a butcher of Roan, in Normandy, who was took up next morning by three fishermen into their boat after a cold frosty night's shipwreck, and with much ado recovered and lived twenty years after.*

*There were in the ship 140 military men, 50 sailors and many noblemen and women (including) William and Richard, the two sons of Henry I, Maude, daughter of Henry I, Richard Earl of chester and his young wife Maude together-er with his 'bastard brother', Othuerus (who was the Royal Tutor)... in all 160 persons (of nobility).*

Thomas, the ship's master, inadvertently guided the vessel onto the notorius rocks in the English Channel known as *'Le Raz de Catteville'* Prince William escaped in a small boat but was distressed by the cries of his half sister Maude, still aboard the sinking ship. He returned for her and died in a brave rescue attempt. The sole survivor was Berold, the butcher, who clung to the sail ropes of the stricken ship. After King Henry learned of the disaster it is said he never smiled again. Intriguingly, Stephen, cousin of the drowned princes, decided at the last moment not to take passage on the White Ship and went on to claim the English throne. Ranulph Meshines became the next earl of Chester. Ranulph always stayed loyal to King Henry I, even when there was rebellion in Normandy

# A Victorian Cemetery

## The Old Cemetery

Immediately opposite the Little Roodee across the river is the Victorian or Old Cemetery, which was laid out in 1848-50 for the Chester General Cemetery Company by a Mr Lister. The cemetery was designed by Thomas Mainwaring Penson, and was most attractively landscaped. Today it is overgrown and has become a haven for plants and wildlife of all sorts.

The once highly picturesque formal layout, with trees and shrubs, winding footpaths and a lake with swans, is an early example of the park-like burial grounds favoured by the Victorians. In the cemetery were a Nonconformist chapel beside a lake, a circular temple and an Anglican chapel in the Norman style on the high ground. A great variety of Victorian monuments remain, but all the buildings have gone and the lake has been drained. Thomas Hughes, the Victorian local historian noted that:

*Nature and Art have combined to produce here a retreat worthy of the dead, and yet full of beauty and allurement for the living.*

Over the many decades of its long life the old cemetery has become a treasury of unusual and fascinating tales of life and death; some tragic and some even humorous. There are so many of these tales that Mr Len Morgan, respected local historian and guide, runs very popular conducted tours of the cemetery.

However, once the sun sinks below the horizon, the *retreat* takes on an eerie, gothic and grotesque appearance that would not be out of place in a story by Edgar Allan Poe. The cemetery is set in a deep, dark hollow. In the threatening half light, little bats can be seen flitting between the gravestones, while strange and unfamiliar sounds utter from the blackness.

## The Chewing Gum Girl (see frontispiece)

On the 13th November 1869, Mabel Frances Ireland-Blackburn died at the tender age of three and a half years. On her sad little grave is a beautiful and peaceful carving, in white marble, of a small sleeping infant. She is known locally has the Chewing Gum Girl, a story made up to discourage children from swallowing chewing gum. Actually she died of whooping cough! This poem used to be near her gravestone:

*Chewing gum - chewing gum - made of wax*
*Brought me to my grave at last.*
*When I die, God will say,*
*"Throw that dirty stuff away!"*

## The Man who made his Own Coffin

William Biddulph Cross was a remarkable man who died on the 5th September 1908, aged 85 years. He was a shoemaker and an electrician, and he possessed a wonderful library. He bound his own books and framed pictures. He was also known for his galvanic cures (stimulation by electric current) and he was a student of anatomy, with many diagrams hanging in his room. However, the thing he was most famous for was - making his own coffin!

*Local historian, Len Morgan, beside the gravestone of*
*William Biddulph Cross*
*Photo: Mike Penney*

110

His coffin took him ten years to complete, and it was made out of thousands of matchboxes packed with wood and framed in black wood. In a space in the lid of the coffin was a battery, with wires and zinc plates throughout the coffin (presumably with the intention of fitting a light). During the two days the coffin was at Messrs. Dutton and Sons, of Frodsham Street, undertakers, the shop was visited by hundreds of interested people keen to have a look at the strange curiosity.

The funeral took place on a wet Wednesday afternoon and, long before the hearse left the deceased's house in Crook Street, hundreds of people crowded on the Rows in Watergate Street and Bridge Street to get a better view. Wreaths were hung on the hearse while the coffin with the battery on the lid was in full view. At the cemetery large crowds lined the path to the grave. Several policemen were on duty to control the crowds but everyone kept good order. The battery was disconnected and removed before the remains were laid to rest and the crowds quietly dispersed at the end of the service.

## Supermum

Mary Jonas, who died on the 4th December 1899, aged 85, was the mother of *thirty-three* children! She gave birth to fifteen sets of twins, each pair a boy and a girl, and three single births. All the babies survived to be christened, but most died before reaching adulthood. Ten were still alive at her husband's death on 24th February 1892. Mary entered a competition promoted by a London magazine called Titbits, to find the lady most contributing to the population of the British Empire, and of course, she won it hands down! The prize was a free copy of the magazine for life.

***Mary Jonas (Supermum)***
*Photo Mike Penney*

*Monument to Doctor William Makepeace Thackery*
*Photo: Mike Penney*

## The Uncle of the Novelist Thackery

Near to the centre of the cemetery are a stone box and a slender spire, which were donated by citizens of Chester, to honour Dr William Makepeace Thackery in recognition of his *abundant kindness* as a doctor and his generous gifts to Chester Infirmary and the Bluecoat School charities. He died in 1849, aged eighty, and was buried in the Cathedral nave before the cemetery opened. He was the uncle of the famous William Makepeace Thackery who wrote the classic novels, and whose somewhat stormy life ended in 1863, at the age of fifty-one.

## The Cuckold

Edward Langtrey was the former husband of the Victorian actress Lillie Langtrey, known worldwide as the Jersey Lilly (because she was born in the island of Jersey and was a mistress of King Edward VII).

Langtrey died in the old Chester Lunatic Asylum on the 16th October 1897, as a result of head injuries received through falling down some steps on board ship in the Irish Sea. He was seen early on Sunday morning wandering the streets of Crewe. Later in the day he was found on the railway line in a dangerous position with his face badly injured. The police medical examiner certified him as not responsible for his own actions, and had him taken to Chester Lunatic Asylum where he died the following Saturday.

The death certificate stated that he died from head injuries that

**Gravestone of Edward Langtrey**

*Photo: Mike Penney*

caused pressure of blood on his brain. During the inquest, the evidence suggested that Langtrey had not been drunk when the accident happened, but it was supposed the divorce proceedings had bothered Langtrey so much that they contributed to the sad train of events that ended in his death. The funeral service, which was held in the cemetery chapel, was only attended by a few of Langtrey's relatives and friends, including a sister-in-law and her husband. However, there were many spectators hoping to see the beautiful Jersey Lilly, but she never turned up. Instead, she sent a wreath and money for funeral expenses and had a statement read saying that she had still been giving Edward Langtrey a quarterly allowance. Lillie died in Monte Carlo in 1929 and was buried besides her parents in her birthplace, St Saviors, Jersey. She died a very rich lady with a string of her own racehorses.

*Stone to Mr & Mrs Christmas*

*Photo: Mike Penney*

## Mr and Mrs (Father) Christmas and Others

Believe it or not, Mr and Mrs Christmas are buried here. Christmas was their surname and they came from Ellesmere Port, not the North Pole. Another stone reminds us of Fireman John Trainer; there is also an inscription, on the gravestone, to his son who was washed overboard from the ship the *City Berlin* on 25th March 1882 aged 23. Ironically, the death of his grandson is also recorded, having died on board the *SS Campania,* on the 8th January 8th January 1911, also aged 23 and buried at sea. Another gravestone records the death of Thomas Owen Hughes, aged 43, who lost his life on 7th May 1913, through the sinking of *RMS Lusitania* in the Great War.

*Memorial for Fireman John Trainer, his son and grandson*

*Photo: Mike Penney*

## Bigwigs

There are many Chester Victorian 'notaries' buried in the cemetery including Prof. Robert Newstead, the renowned archaeologist who excavated many Roman remains in Chester. There are the graves of two of Chester's most famous architects: Thomas Meakin Lockwood and John Douglas. Lockwood was a pupil of Penson, and the most notable examples of his work are the buildings at the corners of Bridge Street and the Cross (1888), Old Bank Buildings (1895), and Owen Owens, Eastgate Street (1900). Douglas, the most prolific of Chester architects, designed Gothic churches and chapels, in brick as well as in stone (St Paul's Church in Boughton, and the Baptist Chapel in Grosvenor Park Road). He was also a leading figure in the black-and-white revival of the later 19th century, and his early work includes the Grosvenor Park Lodge and the south side of St Werburgh Street.

William Brown was buried here in 1852. He was the eldest son of Susannah, founder of the famous Browns of Chester store. Traders and shopkeepers of years gone by include Clemence, Bott, and Bolland (supplier of cakes to the Royal House).

Near to the Grosvenor Road entrance is the first grave dug in the cemetery, that of William Aynton in November 1850. Just above the gate is an over-the-top monument to Henry Raikes, who was buried in 1852. He was Chancellor of Chester, and his effigy can be seen lying close to the ground with a huge stone canopy over it, now overgrown with vegetation.

*Carving of Grosvenor Bridge*

*Photo: Mike Penney*

116

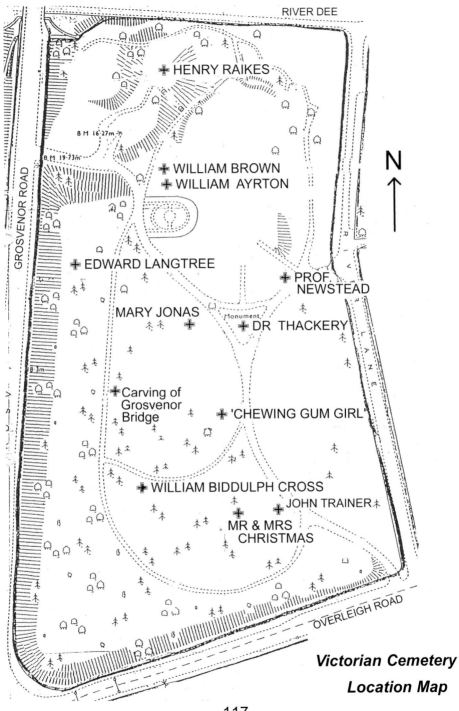

RIVER DEE

GROSVENOR ROAD

B M 16·27m

B M 19·73m

+ HENRY RAIKES

+ WILLIAM BROWN
+ WILLIAM AYRTON

N
↑

+ EDWARD LANGTREE

+ PROF. NEWSTEAD

MARY JONAS
+

Monument

+ DR THACKERY

B·3m

+ Carving of Grosvenor Bridge

+ 'CHEWING GUM GIRL'

+ WILLIAM BIDDULPH CROSS

+ JOHN TRAINER

+ MR & MRS CHRISTMAS

OVERLEIGH ROAD

*Victorian Cemetery*

*Location Map*

*The Chester & Holyhead Railway Bridge Accident*
*24th May 1847*
*From the Illustrated London News*

# The Chester Railway Bridge Disaster of 1847

## The Stephenson's

The success of the steam locomotive was very much a personal triumph for George Stephenson (1781-1848) and his son Robert (1803-1859). As early as 1814, George had built his first steam locomotive. In 1825, George engineered the first public railway on which steam locomotion was used, although initially only on a small scale. The locomotive Active pulled the first train 27 miles along the Stockton-Darlington line, starting from Shildon.

Trials began at Rainhill near Liverpool, in 1829, for a locomotive for use on the Liverpool and Manchester Railway. The five entrants were the Rocket, Cycloped, Sans Pareil, Perseverance and Novelty, with Stephenson's Rocket being the winner. In 1830, the Stephenson's built the Liverpool & Manchester Railway: the first railway to carry passengers and the first to be completely steam-worked from the beginning. Whilst attending the opening of the line, the politician William Huskisson was knocked down and killed by Stephenson's Rocket, highlighting the dangers of the new technology.

Nevertheless, the Stephenson's were on the crest of the railway age and were unrivalled as railway engineers in the early 1830s:

> *It was their appreciation that one day all local lines would be joined together in a nationwide network that led to the adoption of a standard gauge of track throughout most of the country.*

## Railway Mania

Railways were costly to build and they became an engineer's paradise, with lavish standards of finish to major bridges and viaducts, tunnel portals and stations but, as Neil Cossons explains in *The BP Book of Industrial Archaeology:*

> *There were real reasons, however, for the heroic quality of much railway engineering and architecture, particularly in the late 1830s and early 1840s.*
>
> *Firstly, engineers such as the Stephenson's and Brunel, while consciously designing for the future, had to allow for the limited locomotive tractive effort and relatively underdeveloped mechanical knowledge of their day. So they built lines with easy gradients and therefore committed themselves to building heavy earthworks.*
>
> *Secondly, there was the problem of making the railway a socially acceptable means of travel, and this was solved by magnificent termini, architecturally acceptable in a city environment, line-side stations of a vernacular or domestic style often beautifully attuned to their geographical and social surroundings, and major engineering structures handled with a panache and yet sympathy for landscape unequalled to this day.*
> *Euston or Temple Meads had the same function as the airline terminals of today, being designed not merely to book the passenger on the train but to inflate his ego, enhance the prestigiousness of the railway experience, and reassure him that all was not dangerous.*

## Chester Steam

The 1840s saw the building of many thousands of miles of railway track. The first railways came to Chester in 1840, when a line was opened from Chester to Birkenhead and, a month later, one from Chester to Crewe. In 1846 Chester was connected with Ruabon. By 1848 the Chester and Holyhead Railway had reached Bangor and various branch lines were opened soon after. From 1840 to 1848 a temporary station was used to the north of the present General Station. The latter was built between 1847 and 1848. Its architects were C.H. Wild and Francis Thompson; the contractor was Thomas Brassey, now celebrated by memorials on Chester Station and in the Cathedral. There is no doubt whatsoever that this station was designed to enhance the prestigiousness of the railway experience and reassure the passenger that railways were safe.

Brian Harris in *Bartholomew City Guides  Chester* states that:

> *The station has always been regarded as a significant contribution to the city's architecture. Its facade is of brick, with stone dressings; the detailing is Classical, in an Italianate style.*
> *Its great size was dictated by its need to accommodate not only a large number of trains but also the administrative offices of the railway companies using it.*

So with all this tremendous time, effort and money spent to reassure the public that the railways were safe, it must have come as a devastating shock to Robert Stephenson, engineer to the Chester & Holyhead Railway (C.H.R), to learn of the collapse of the bridge over the River Dee: the bridge that he had designed. The accident could not have happened at worse time for Stephenson. The construction of the Conwy and Menai tubular bridges was just starting, and he was about to stand as a candidate for Parliament:

> *A blow fell upon Stephenson, which for lesser men might have had graver consequences.*
> *The Dee Bridge, for the design of which he was responsible, failed.*

## Cast Iron

The original intention had been for a brick bridge, completing the brick viaduct approach to the river, one and a half miles from Chester. At an early date, however, Stephenson substituted a design of three cast iron spans of 98 ft (30 metres) each, on a 51 degree skew to the river. The iron spans rested on stone abutments and two stone piers. Each railway line was supported between the piers on two parallel 107 ft - 6 in (33 metres) cast iron composite girders in three sections joined by semi-circular castings secured to their upper flanges. Connecting the composite girders were thirteen wrought iron tie bars.

The fatal design error was that each set of girders was independent from its neighbour alongside. Although connected together, the girders could move both sideways and vertically independently of each other; so that the tie bars became weakened through constant twisting and turning. With the line on a curve and the girders being on the skew, the load did not bear uniformly and produced a rocking motion. Also, the load being on one side only of the bottom flange of the girders, there was an outward thrust at the bottom which drew the two tops together by as much as 2 inches for 48 tons, imparting a twisting motion or torsional strain to the girders and tie rods.

In consequence, when the accident occurred, the thirteen lateral ties had all been either torn from their sockets or wrenched off near the sockets of the girder left standing and the cast iron girder fractured in mid-span. In addition, as the reader may be aware, cast iron is strong in compression but relatively weak in tension and torsion, so that cast iron was a totally unsuitable material to use for this application.

## *The Accident*

All seemed well when one track of the bridge was opened in September 1846 for use by contractors. On one occasion three engines and tenders, together weighing 90 tons, passed over without any apparent damage. Since November 1846 the bridge had been in regular use by the trains of the Shrewsbury and Chester Railway (S.C.R).

On the 24th May 1847 the southern girder on the western span of the bridge broke as the 6.15 pm S.C.R train from Chester to Ruabon was passing over it. The train was running five minutes late and at an estimated speed of 30 mph. As the engine ran over the last span of the bridge the driver felt a sudden and unusual vibration and heard a peculiar noise. Realising something was dreadfully wrong he slammed his regulator handle wide open to accelerate the train off the bridge. Although the engine got across, dragging its derailed tender with it, the carriages fell with a tremendous crash 36 ft (11 meters) into the river below. The tender broke away from the engine hurling the fireman into the river and killing him. The guard in the leading van and two coachmen travelling with him were killed, together with a passenger. Another passenger died sometime after the accident. Eight passengers were injured.

## The Aftermath

At the coroner's inquest early in June 1847, evidence was heard from workmen on the bridge of vibration and girder deflection when trains passed over, and the inference was that they (the girders) were unsafe. Stephenson, in his evidence, said that he saw nothing to *indicate weakness or imperfection in the bridge works*. The hearing was adjourned to allow time for the Commissioners of Railways to report on the accident, and their report in June 1847 was critical of the design of the bridge.

***Broken span at the Dee Bridge***

*From the Illustrated London News*

The resumed coroner's inquest then came to its verdict:

*That the girder broke because it was of insufficient strength
to bear the pressure of quick trains passing over it.*

As there were upwards of a hundred other cast iron bridges, either built or contemplated on the railways in the country at this time, a government inquiry was called for to reassure the public of the safety of this type of bridge: a commission was appointed in August 1847 *to inquire into the Application of Iron to Railway Structures.* The Dee Bridge figured largely in the evidence of the commission's investigations. A method of strengthening the girders of cast iron railway bridges was hurriedly applied to similar bridges throughout the railway system following publication of the commissions findings in July 1849.

During the following years the use of compound cast iron girders almost completely ceased, and bridges were either further strengthened or reconstructed. In the case of the Dee Bridge the structure was extensively rebuilt in brick and wrought iron in 1870-71. However, it was not until the Norwood Junction accident on the Brighton line in 1891, that all remaining cast iron underline bridges were finally replaced.

Although Robert Stephenson had not come out of the inquiry unscathed, his magnificent and accomplished triumphs of the Conwy and Menai wrought iron tubular bridges was to overshadow the Dee Bridge tragedy. To be certain of safety, Stephenson had a one-sixth scale model of one of the tubes tested to destruction before the eventual design was arrived at and construction of the Menai Bridge and its smaller neigbour at Conwy. Conwy was built first, as the tubes were smaller and only had to be raised about 5 metres, which proved a useful trial for the much grander Menai Bridge. These bridges were important landmarks in the evolution of civil engineering, because they marked the first use of the beam principle for a long span bridge.

Luckily for him, Stephenson's standing in the country had not suffered over the Dee Bridge disaster; the electors of Whitby confidently returned him as their MP on 30th July, an office he was to hold, as a Conservative and Protectionist, until his death.

# The Old City Hospital

## *From Pauper to Patient*

The old City Hospital is, without a doubt, reputed to be the most haunted and spookiest place in Chester. It had a long history of haunting and, over many years, there have been endless reports of sightings and eerie happenings from staff, patients and visitors.

The Hospital was originally the old Workhouse that opened in 1878. The Workhouse consisted of five large blocks of red brick buildings, designed to house 500 paupers. In 1892, the Workhouse consisted of the Workhouse itself, a hospital and a chapel dedicated to St. James the Less, which was consecrated in 1880. The grassed area around this chapel was used as a graveyard for at least 1,350 burials between 1880 and 1900. By 1930, the Workhouse complex had grown to eight blocks covering an enormous site of 12 acres.

On the main block was a tall water tower. Capping it was a spire crowned with a spike that could be seen from a great distance. This spike was a beacon to tramps to say that here was a meal and refuge for at least one night. That is why, amongst gentlemen of the road, workhouses were called the spike.

**The Chapel of St James the Less**
*Photo: Mike Penney*
124

*Burial Mound*
*Photo: Mike Penney*

In the 1950s, the City Hospital expanded considerably. Following the opening of the Nucleus Hospital, off the Liverpool Road in 1983, the City Hospital ceased to be a general hospital and specialised in Geriatrics until it closed in 1991. The Hospital buildings were demolished in the same year and the site is now covered with a housing estate. Physically, at least, only the chapel and cemetery remain.

## The Upside Down Cross

The chapel ceased to be used for services in 1948 and, after falling into disrepair, was de-consecrated in 1951. In the chapel graveyard there are two mass burials, probably dug when there was an epidemic. However, most graves are three or five to a plot, with at least two or three triple deckers, where there are twelve bodies buried in one communal grave; two side by side and six deep. It is said that on a cold frosty day the burial mounds can still be seen clearly.

125

Only one gravestone remains; the inscription on it reads:

SACRED
TO THE MEMORY OF
THE PERSONS
BURIED IN THIS GROUND

*Remaining gravestone*
*Photo: Roy Wilding*

Another gravestone is said to have also existed: to mark where the poor illegitimate babies of the workhouse inmates were buried. The little souls were all buried together in a pit which was marked by this gravestone, on top of which was an upside down cross, to mark the supposed stigma of their illegitimacy. The incidence of illegitimate babies dying was very high in the workhouse and, under the brutally harsh rules of those places, they were not allowed burial in a Christian graveyard, and had to be buried beyond consecrated ground.

## Pit-A-Pat

It was the end of a long day and the Sister was very tired after looking after some very ill patients. It was a late autumn evening and an icy cold wind blew through the old trees that had stood for decades by the side of the old ward. She was about to go off duty and decided to use the back stairs leading from the ward to the ground floor, which had once connected the old workhouse wards.

It was very dark on the stairs. As the Sister got halfway down them, she heard the sound of light footsteps climbing the stairs towards her; the lightest of tread, like the footsteps of a young child. She stopped on the stairs and waited to see who was coming towards her. Suddenly she felt something cold surround her. A chill wind ruffled her hair and she felt the light touch of little cold fingers on her wrist.

She was also aware of a musty smell, like the smell of newly turned earth. The footsteps stopped. Then immediately they started going up the stairs behind her. In the morning a check was made. Patches of damp soil and moss were discovered on the stairs; the trail of debris led to the entrance of the old graveyard.

## The Quick and the Dead

One night just before Christmas, a man who live in Hoole was taking a short-cut through the hospital grounds to get home. The short-cut lay through a tree-lined walk by the side of the old chapel. The walk was always very dark, particularly at night. On this particular night there was no moon out, but he could still make out the old chapel standing grim and stark.

All of a sudden he felt an icy cold shiver run down his spine. As he turned his head he thought he saw a shadowy figure leaning over one of the graves just in front of the chapel. He hesitated for an instance. Then he kept on walking. As he neared the grave, he continued to look at the figure. It seemed to be tearing at something in the ground.

The soil had been disturbed and he shouted at the figure: a woman dressed in flowing black robes. She turned towards him. He saw that she was faceless; just an empty blackness in the hood where the face should be.

It is said that he reached his home in record time and never used that short cut again!

127

# The Man in the Brown Suit

Some people on the verge of death seem to experience dead loved ones coming to assist them on their journey to the unknown. Whether this is due to hallucinations or not who knows? However, Charles Fairclough in *Chester Ghosts and Poltergeists* records one event where a visitation was witnessed by at least four other people:

*It was a January night in 1976, I was a trainee nurse at the time, in Chester City Hospital. There were four of us, and our duty room was adjacent to a four-bedded cubicle ward. Among our patients was a lady who was seriously ill and about whom we were quite concerned. So we decided to call in the doctor. While waiting for the doctor whom we knew would not be available for some twenty minutes, we had a cup of tea. From where we sat we had a view down the corridor; suddenly a man dressed in a brown suit was seen approaching; we couldn't guess his age, he just came walking down the corridor towards us, passing the open doorway of our room which as I said was adjacent to the ward door.*

*He just passed by and went into the sick ward. Upon this I said to the ward sister, "My! He might have had the good manners to acknowledge us". "Yes, he could have done," replied the sister. Then I added, "I suppose I'll have to go and see him." We all thought he was a doctor. So I got up and went into the cubicle, but to my surprise there was no one there - that is, besides the patients. I came out and said in a surprised tone to my colleagues, "He's not there!" My colleagues looked up and replied tartly, "Don't be stupid Jackson, he must be there!" Then I went back to the ward, gazed around and returning to my colleagues said, "But he's not"! With that the sister came out and looked into the ward, then said, " Oh! Go away Jackson, you've got me as confused as yourself!"*

*Well we were all giggly about it as it was so unexpected. Anyway, a short time passed and the doctor arrived, and we said to him, "Has one of your colleagues been to see the lady?" "No," replied the doctor, "I haven't sent anyone". Well, he examined the lady and remarked that she would be all right and departed. We had no other occurrences during the night and in the morning when we went to wash the lady, she said to us, "Did you see my son last night?" Upon hearing that remark we looked at each other knowingly*

*and replied, "No."*
*The lady added, "I knew he'd come to visit me, he's a lovely boy, he looked so*
*smart in his brown suit,"*
*We said, "Oh!" Then I asked the lady, "Does your son live with you?"*
*"Oh no!" replied the lady, "He was killed during the war"*
*Then she repeated over and over again, "He's a lovely boy, a lovely boy, and*
*he looked so smart in his brown suit."*
*My colleague and I just looked at each other, for it seemed obvious that*
*she was referring to the apparition we had seen during the night*
*going in to visit his mother.*
*Sad to relate but that lady died around lunch time that day.*

## It's coming to get me!

On the 20th February 1959, a young man had been to visit his wife and new born baby in the city hospital, but because of an outbreak of flu, neither fathers nor relatives were allowed to enter the hospital. All they could do was stand shivering outside the hospital and gaze up at the windows in the hope of seeing their loved ones.

However, the new father was so happy and, almost in a dream, decided to make his way home through Hoole. What happened next was so terrifying that the young man had to warn others of his nightmare experience in the Chester Observer:

*I strolled through Hoole in a dream, enjoying both the casualness*
*of the walk and my new status of father. For no apparent reason,*
*I found myself on the canal path near Griffith's old flour mill...*
*It was then that I saw it. What appeared to be a pale grey figure*
*rose slowly out of the canal. It constantly twisted and changed into*
*a variety of sinister shapes, sometimes transparent, sometimes opaque.*
*Slowly, but deliberately, it drifted on the surface of the water and rolled*
*on to the path. I was absolutely petrified. I tried to scream,*
*but not a sound came. Above all, I wanted to run, but I stayed to the ground.*
*It seemed I was paralysed. The ghostly form advanced slowly,*
*its shape still constantly changing...*

*I was so hypnotised by the shape that I could only look at it...*
*With a sudden swirl it was all around me.I was completely enveloped in a*
*cold, clammy, intangible vapour. I have never been so frightened in all my life.*
*Suddenly my sense of survival returned. I let out one ear shattering scream*
*and bolted along the canal path. I came to a halt halfway up George Street*
*when I realised that the figures I was bumping into were real [people])....*

# A Host of Hauntings

Almost all of the wards were believed to be haunted, but Ward 21 was considered to be the most haunted one in the whole hospital. It is said that the *lady in grey* appeared almost every night in this ward. She was a small figure in grey nun like robes, who glided down the corridor and straight through the double doors at the end of the ward. Nurses on duty were always hearing footsteps in this ward, but there was never anybody there.

The haunting became so bad that it was decided to close the ward and take the opportunity to carry out some refurbishment work. One of the cleaning ladies had to go up to the empty ward to get some bags. She unlocked the entrance door and started to make her way through the ward. Halfway down the corridor were a pair of closed double doors that all of a sudden threw wide open of their own accord. The cleaner thought that someone was playing a trick on her, and stepped through them, but much to her terror they slammed shut behind her. She fled from that ward and would never enter it again!

An exorcism was performed on ward 21, but this only made matters worse, for the grey lady did not rest in peace for long. In fact almost as soon as the ward was reopened she appeared again, but this time she started to groan loudly as she passed through the ward. She was seen by nurses to appear through the wall by the main door into the ward. To begin with all that could be seen were a pair of hands which appeared through the wall and remained there for about two minutes, then gradually the rest of her appeared. Her cowl always covered her face and no one ever saw her features. She would press the buzzer at the top of the long corridor and pulled the bell push so that the patient red light came on. It is said that no one was able to photograph this ward because only blank negatives would be the result.

Ward 20 also had a particularly bad reputation for being haunted. One lady patient recalled that as she got out of bed one night at about 3 a.m, when the ward was very quite, she could see a figure coming towards her. At first she thought it was one of the nurses, but as the form came nearer she saw that figure was all dressed in grey crinoline with the skirt standing out stiffly around her. Above the skirt was a grey shawl and she had on a little grey bonnet. In her hand she was carrying something that resembled a lamp. However, the patient did not feel any fear of the apparition and went to speak to it, but the figure glided past and disappeared. Although the lady realised that she had seen a ghost, she still felt no fear and just got back into bed and went to sleep. Apparently this ghost was a frequent visitor on the ward and her presence had comforted everyone who had seen her.

Ward 20 had a balcony leading out from the main ward and this overlooked the car park; it was known as the jumpers' balcony because of the number of people who had tried to commit suicide by jumping off it, in most cases ending their lives. One such patient, on learning that he had a terminal illness, threw himself off the balcony with fatal results. A short time later it was notice by the hospital staff that a pool of blood had formed on the roadway, and this was cleared up by the porters. However, every time they cleared the blood up, it would reappear almost at once. Countless treatments were given to clear the blood away and eventually the blood did not reappear, but left a large bloodstain etched into the roadway which remained until the closure of the hospital. The balcony doors were also said to open of their own accord with a thunderous crash and boxes were jammed against them to keep them closed, but they still slammed open.

And what of the present? It is said that there are still goings-on in and around the old chapel and graveyard.

# The Gaumont Ghost

## The Picture Palace

The grand opening of the Gaumont Cinema took place on Monday 2nd March 1931. The main half-timbered entrance of the cinema still exists in the present Bingo Hall, just off Cow Lane Bridge.

**Gaumont Cinema**
*Photo courtesy of Vincent Dunning  & David A Ellis*

As in keeping with a 1930's Picture Palace, the entrance hall was:

> *Reminiscent of the large hall of an Italian Palace,*
> *with a blue and gold ceiling relieved in red.*

On one side of the entrance hall were the grand stairs to the balcony and the Oak Restaurant. On the other side was a grand canopied fireplace. The expansive auditorium was fan-shaped, and could seat 1,200 people on the ground floor. The proscenium opening was 15 metres wide by 9 metres high, and was surrounded by a ribbed lighting cove. A huge ornamented dome was set in the centre of the main ceiling.

The Gaumont also acted as a theatre, where many shows were held over the years. It had a large 9 metre deep stage, and nine dressing rooms.

Entertainment at the Gaumont ranged from the Liverpool Philharmonic, to Bill Haley and the Comets.

The cinema housed a magnificent theatre organ, arranged in two chambers above the proscenium arch. The organist played popular music in the intervals between films, while ice creams and refreshment were sold. In addition, more than 200 recitals of popular music were broadcast over the radio in the 1930s.

By 1954, CinemaScope had arrived, and a 12 metre wide screen was installed which could be flown (raised), so that the stage could be used fully. The 1960s saw the decline in cinemas, and the Gaumont closed in 1961. The interior of the building was stripped, and the organ removed for spares and scrap. Within the shell of the two levels, a 24-lane bowling alley was formed. However, soon after, the Gaumont was altered again and became the present Bingo Hall.

## *The Phantom of the Theatre*

It is a tradition that a theatre should have a theatre ghost, and while Chester has had many theatres throughout the ages, it is a surprise to discover that the Gaumont is the only Chester theatre reputed to have a ghost, with reported hauntings from as early as the Second World War until at least the 1980s.

During the Second World War two projectionists were in the Gaumont's projection box when they heard one loud thud followed by two small thuds on the roof of the box. As this was when an air raid was taking place, the projectionists thought that a German had baled out of his aircraft and landed on the roof. The thuds sounded like a body dropping followed immediately by the legs hitting the roof. The roof was searched but nothing was found. This happened many times, always during an air raid, but nothing was ever found.

(Author's note: according to a lady usherette working at the Gaumont in the 1940s, she remembers that the building was infested with huge rats, possible from the adjoining canal, perhaps these had got onto the roof and made the thudding sounds).

In the same projection box were three rooms: the main room, the re-winding room and a small room with doors leading to the other two rooms. During one show, the first projectionist was in the main room running the projectors, and his assistant was in the film re-winding room. The first projectionist turned from the projector and looked towards a small window in the third room. He was shocked to see the face of a man looking at him. He was certain that it

133

# ★ GAUMONT PALACE ★
## — Chester's Wonder Cinema. —

**ALL WEEK** commencing **MARCH 9th.**

SONG, ROMANCE
and COLOUR
COMBINED IN ONE GLORIOUS MASTERPIECE,

# "THE
# VAGABOND
# KING,"

WITH
## DENNIS KING and Jeanette MacDonald.

ROWLAND H. CUTLER at the Mighty Compton Organ.

FREE CAR PARK. | OAK CAFE and RESTAURANT.

PRICES; 8d., 1/-, 1/3 and 1/6.
Sats. and Bank Holidays, after 4 p.m.,
8d., 1/-, 1/6 and 2/-.

No Half-Prices after
4 p.m. on Saturdays.

*Cinema Poster from the first film shown at the Gaumont*

was not his own reflection in the glass, or light from the projector playing
tricks. He sent his assistant into the small room through one door while he
went in through the other. It was impossible for anyone to get out without
passing either man (the only window opened to a drop of about eighty feet).
On entering, the room was completely empty.

# Bowled Over

In mid-winter 1964, two bowling alley mechanics finished work at about two am, having seen the Midnight League finish their last game. It was a terrible night. A blizzard blew outside. Road conditions were dreadful, with ice and snow. The men were unable to get home on their motor bikes. So the only option was to spend a comfortable and secure night in the empty, but locked, bowling alley:

*My mate decided he would make a cup of coffee before turning in;*
*meanwhile I had a wash. My mate was in the workshop and I was*
*having my wash in the staff room, about fifteen yards from the workshop.*
*There was a crash, and I thought, 'There go the cups'.*
*I ran onto the old stage of the cinema, which after re-development*
*had been left as no use could be made of it. On the stage*
*I met my mate who was on his way to see what I had dropped.*
*We laughed and said it must have been George and went back to*
*what we had been doing.*

Within seconds of getting back to the washroom, there was a second crash that came from the stage. Both men ran back onto the dimly lit stage. In the centre of the stage they saw a broken sheet of glass, which they thought had fallen from a window in the scenery flies high above them. They looked up and could see something or someone moving. They called up that it was very dangerous to be at that height, but there was no answer.

The two men thought that the headlights of a car from outside might have caused the light moving across the flies. However, the thing moved back towards a vertical iron ladder that was bolted to the wall. The light started to move slowly down the rungs just as if someone was shining a torch on the ladder. Having reached the stage, the light passed through an open door and into a passage, and out of sight. At this point the men telephoned the police, who soon arrived:

*An inspector and a sergeant confronted my mate and myself.*
*When we had finished, the inspector told the sergeant to climb*
*the ladder to the top and see if he could find anything.*
*I don't know if the sergeant was afraid of heights or what,*
*but he refused to climb the ladder. At this, the inspector radioed*
*for a dog and handler, and they arrived and were told our story.*
*The inspector asked us to show him where the passage led*
*that the light went into. This was also part of the old cinema*
*and led to the now disused and empty dressing rooms in which*

*the stars used to change. Having passed through the passage*
*we entered the small building by the only unlocked door.*
*There were three rooms on the ground floor, three on the first floor,*
*and one room built in the attic.*

*As these rooms were not in use, there were no lights, so*
*the police torches were the only illumination. The inspector told*
*the dog handler to go in first with his dog.*
*This he did with us all following behind.*
*The dog led the way and sniffed around in all the rooms on the*
*ground floor and the first floor. But when he came to the attic*
*he refused to pass through the door and even though the handler*
*pulled on the lead the dog cried and cowered away, the hair on its back*
*standing on end. The inspector rushed into the room followed by*
*the sergeant but it was completely empty. The dog still refused to enter...*

The something or someone was never found.

## The Man in the Tweed Suit

All through the 1970s and 80s there were continual sightings of the ghost
throughout the theatre: in the Tudor Room, in the upper ceiling void, on the
stairs, in fact all over the place. Two such sightings refer to the man in the
tweed suit:

*1973.*
*Mr. Jones, an assistant manager employed at the club, a man of*
*rather cynical, disbelieving attitude, especially [to] anything connected*
*with the supernatural... He had gone to the bottom of an exit where*
*there was a storeroom, to collect a box of plastic cups.*
*He turned the corner at the bottom of the exit and upon entering*
*the doorway to the storeroom, he observed that the door was ajar.*
*He also noticed on entering a man, dressed in a tweed jacket*
*standing only a few feet from him, walk behind a pile of cartons.*
*After glancing at him, Mr. Jones challenged the identification*
*of this man... walked to the pile of boxes and peered round.*
*To his amazement, there was no one there!*
*There was no other place in the storeroom where one could hide,*
*and the only way in or out was through the one and only door*
*he'd just walked through!*

In 1978, a lady cleaner was sweeping the stairs near to the same exit, when
she was startled to feel something brush against her as she bent to pick up

her dustpan. She looked up to see a man, dressed in a tweed jacket, silently walk past her and disappear around the corner. She ran to the top of the exit quite shaken, and with the help of her colleagues they searched the exit area and also the buffet storeroom, but found no sign of anyone. No one could have left the building in that area as the exit door was locked.

## The Ghost Speaks

In 1983, a painting and decorating firm were redecorating the building interior. Eight men were employed working throughout the night so as not to interfere with the running of the club. One painter, who specialised in ornamental decorating, was painting the ornamental ceiling in the Tudor Room:

*At about 2 am he was busy on the top of some scaffolding*
*when he heard a voice call out, "Why don't you keep this door shut!"*
*and the door leading to the manager's office,*
*situated mid-way in the room, slammed shut.*
*Thinking that one of his mates was larking about, he descended*
*from the scaffold and reopened the office door.*
*To his amazement, there was no one inside.*
*He ran down the stairs and found that all seven of his mates*
*were busy engaged in decorating in various parts of the stalls area,*
*which was a considerable distance from where he was working.*
*A check of the premises revealed no sign of any one else.*

(Author's note: the story goes that the ghost was that of one of the cinema managers or projectionists who hanged himself in the projection box some-time in the 1930s, but I have no evidence to substantiate this).

# Barlow's Ghost

## What's Down There?

Mike is a sensible man and a sceptic as far as ghosts go. He likes to have things logically proven before he believes them. However, in the latter half of the nineteen-seventies his scepticism about the supernatural was sorely tested.

*The*
*Old*
*Vaults*
*(Barlows)*

*Photo: Mike*
*Penney*

For just over two years he lived in one of the oldest pubs in Chester. It was his late father's pub, known to locals as 'Barlows'. The real name of the pub was Ye Olde Vaults, Bridge Street. The building is mostly Georgian with much older bits remaining. While he lived there he had experiences which seem to have no logical explanation:

*One busy Saturday afternoon I was working in the ancient sandstone cellar. About three-quarters of the way along the cellar was a brick built partition wall with a very heavy, old wooden door which was always jammed open. As I was changing one of the barrels I heard some noises coming from the far end of the cellar. I thought it was Dad, who I thought had entered the cellar from the other end. I called out to him, but got no reply. So I went to have a look, but did not see anything.*

*My first thoughts were that he was playing a joke on me. Just a few hours earlier an old bar man had been telling us that the pub and cellar were haunted. Anyway, I carried on with my work, and just as I had finished changing the barrels, the old door in the partition wall suddenly slammed shut!*

*I went to see what had happened, but just couldn't open the door. I called out again to (my dad) to stop messing around, but got no reply. I decided to give it up as a bad job and go through the trap door to the downstairs bar. To my surprise, Dad was in the middle of pulling a pint and could not possibly have been in the cellar.*

*I told him what had happened and he laughed and said I was extracting the proverbial. The cellar door, that had slammed shut, had never been closed all the time we had lived there, and almost certainly not for some years before that. The door's rusty old hinges had dropped and its threshold was jammed on the floor. At the end of my shift we went into the cellar, and it took both of us a great deal of effort to prise open the door. It was impossible that the door had been slammed shut by a draft or by human hand! So what did it?*

## The Spirited Ghost

Another happening occurred on a Friday night around midnight, after the pub had closed:

*Only the back lights from the bar were on.*
*Dad, some of the bar staff and myself were sitting in the downstairs bar*
*having a drink and a chat. The subject got round to the age of the pub*
*and its previous landlords. Being interested in local history*
*I was able to tell my companions some history of the building,*
*and of one of its previous landlords in particular: George Barlow,*

*I went on to tell them that, by all accounts, old George was*
*quite a colourful character. He was involved in various activities*
*alongside running Barlows. One was bottling his own brand of whisky*
*at the back of the pub. As I was telling this story to my colleagues,*
*there was a noise behind the bar, and all looked up to see the*
*plastic nameplate, for the brand of whisky we had on optic,*
*fall off to reveal the writing underneath George Barlow*
*Highland Brand Scotch Whisky! No one had been near the*
*optic apart from, perhaps, George Barlow himself?*

## Death's Breath

It was Saturday night and Mike had been telling a few friends about the ghostly happenings in the pub. One drink lead to another and Mike's two sisters suggested a ghost hunt; everyone thought this would be a laugh. Above the pub's flat was another floor, which had not been used for years. It had no electricity, and seemed the ideal place for a ghost hunt:

*So out came the candles and off we set climbing the two flights of stairs*
*to the top of the building. There was a long corridor with three rooms*
*off to the right and a larger room straight ahead which overlooked*
*the main street. George Barlow had used this room as an office.*
*As we walked along the corridor we visited every room calling for George*
*to show himself. At first, there was no reaction.We then entered the end*
*room, and we all stood in the middle calling for George to show himself. One*
*of the party, who was a very sensitive person, was getting very nervous and*
*said that we should return to the lower floors.*

*However, having had quite a few drinks, we continued to ask George to*
*show himself. After about five minutes, we were ready to leave when*
*there was a loud noise, like floorboards creaking, from one of the other rooms.*
*A split second later all our candles went out simultaneously.*
*We were then left to negotiate our way out in utter blackness.*
*Needless to say, we never attempted another ghost hunt.*

## Sitting Tenant

In 2002, the last pint was drawn at Barlows and the old pub closed its doors. Currently the premises are being redeveloped throughout for other purposes than a public house. Big Eddy of Wallasey is leading the team of builders carrying out the renovation work and according to them *it's the queerest place they've ever worked.* Up on the top floor both Eddy and his lads say curtains move all by themselves without a hint of any draft. Something or someone keeps touching them from behind, but when they turn round, the room is empty. One of the worst places to work in is the semi-darkness of the cellar, where the workmen have a very unpleasant sense of an *unseen presence.* One of the electricians said the building is just like a refrigerator and every part is always deathly cold. He said he would be glad to get out of the place. So is Mr Barlow still in residence? Who knows

***St John's churchyard. An eerie place before the inner ring road cut through. (See next chapter.)***

*(Unknown artist)*                    *Courtesy of Simon Warburton*

# The Divine Kiss

## Devouring Goddess

The Roman invaders named Chester: DEVA, after the holy river that embraces the city. Deva means goddess or holy one. Gods and goddess have many facets, and so it was with the lady Deva. She not only gave life with her sacred waters, but also devoured and dragged souls to their watery graves. Of all the hundreds of deaths that were listed in the Chester Coroners' reports, for the period between the early sixteenth and late eighteenth centuries, drowning came out top.

It is easy to forget that, at one time, the river was an integral part of everyday life. As a port, shipping was vital to the city. Industry was based on waterpower. The only bridge across the river, for miles, was the Old Dee Bridge, which was a toll bridge. To avoid the toll or reduce their journey, people would attempt to cross the river at various fords. So it is not surprising that many were drowned. The river was also a convenient place to wash, bathe or even commit suicide.

The River Dee is a fickle place, with shifting sands, treacherous currents and a killer tide. Misjudge the times of the tides or try to cross a ford when a fresh (melt or storm water) is due from the Welsh hills  and you're dead! In particular, horse riders seemed susceptible to drowning, by loosing control of their horses and falling into the river. Some young men went sailing in 1672 and took the river for granted, but paid a terrible price:

*Death of Henry Young. Several young men had gone sailing and got stuck on a bank near Shotwick. They left the boat, one, the examinee (witness at the Coroners' court) got to another vessel, the other three tried to get to Shotwick. Henry Young's body [was] found, the other two [bodies] missing.*

The Dee Mills were important water-powered industrial complexes for hundreds of years, and many workers had accidents associated with the river. In 1748, John Phillips, a carpenter, drowned while making a new salmon cage at the east end of the causeway or weir above the Dee Bridge. Phillips was using a *corrikle (*coracle*)* to gain access to the site of the salmon cage and, for some strange reason, he jumped from his craft when it was halfway across the river, then unsuccessfully attempted to swim to the shore.

In 1773, Thomas Dannald, a baker and also the Clerk of the Chester Waterworks, was killed when:

'He [Dannald] stood upon a plank in the water engine in order to oyl the brasses there he accidentally slipped and fell down headlong under the crank belonging to the said water engine by which he received a mortall wound or was crushed and bruised by the said crank in such a barbarous manner that he instantly dyed.'

Drowning was not limited to the River Dee. Fresh water supply was primitive and many premises had water butts in their back yards. Just as garden ponds today are regarded as a safety risk, so water butts claimed many lives (some by suicide):

*1569: Elizabeth Plumpton, drowned in a tub of water in the backside of a house in Watergate Street.*

## Make Hay

Work and fooling about just don't mix, as Tom Furnival found out to his cost in 1735:

*John Furnival, yeoman; while haymaking on the estate of Sir Thomas Brooke Bart. He suggested that two of his work-mates George Beckett and Daniel Smith should see who could throw a pikell (hay fork) the furthest; while George Beckett was thowing it, one of the grains (prongs) flew out and hit him in the stomach, giving him a wound from which he later died.*

## Whom the Gods Love

The Coroners' reports also record deaths from a variety of causes, and probably the saddest entries in the records are those of children:

*1668: Grace Moire, aged one and a half, daughter of George Moire navigator, fell into the street from Watergate Row (and died).*

*1670: Richard Broster, a child of nine got hold of some rat poison (arsenic) and ate it, thinking it was sugar.*

*1682: Infant child of Elizabeth Evans, born in St John's churchyard, killed by its mother. (See illustration, page 141)*

*1753: 'John Taylor, son of Thomas Taylor of the s$^d$ City Labourer...was going down a Well of Thomas Bingley Alderman...was suffocated by the Damp arising in the s$^d$ Well'.*

## Brutal Masters

In the old days, workers had virtually no rights and were sometimes treated terribly:

*1613: Robert Gardiner, killed by his master in the kitchen with a shredding knife.*

*1615: Lawria Verch Richard, beaten to death by her master, William Parri, shoemaker.*

## Molotov Cocktail

Chester was once one of the most important cities in England. It was a major manufacturing centre, working mainly in the leather industry. It was also a bustling port, with ships plying between Spain, France, Portugal, Ireland, the Baltic countries, and other British ports. In addition, it was a military centre and gateway for troops going to Ireland. Situated near the Welsh border, with numerous markets, fairs, horse races, and up to a hundred small pubs, it's no wonder that there were so many fights, brawls and duels in such a rough and ready environment. Many confrontations often ended in death:

*1733 'Joseph Price mariner, aged 15, died from a blow from Thomas Jump, son of Thomas Jump of Preston brewer, who was trying to stop a fight between Price and John Jones aged 11.'*

*1703: John Liversley, 12 year old son of Robert Liversley, barber, died from a wound in the arm caused by a red hot iron thrown by George Quirk, blacksmith,in Foregate Street.*

## Like a Thief in the Night

Death can strike when we least expect it, and comes without warning:

*1673: Edward Oliver, Thomas Gardiner, William Lloyd, Samuel Bennett, John Jones, James Lloyd, Charles Sunderland, Nicholas Boulton, and Charles Warburton, all labourers, [were] killed when confusion arose as a large number of people, who had gathered at the Common Hall to elect a member for parliament, tried to descend the stairs all at once, and fell on top of each other.*

*1682: Mary Ambrose, spinster, fell into a brewing pan and was scalded to death.*

*1744: Margaret Betson, spinster, killed by part of a roof collapsing on her in bed during a storm at the house of James Percival, sword bearer.*

144

# A Snug Tale

### The Pied Bull, Northgate Street

Many publicans in Chester like to boast that they have their own (ghostly) spirits. However, at the ancient Pied Bull, in Northgate Street, they not only know the name of their very own ghost, but also the exact date when he died. The Pied Bull was once a coaching inn, and from the outside is still an impressive eighteenth century inn, with its upper floor built over the pavement to form an arcade. However, inside the building is much older with an impressive seventeenth century staircase.

On a pillar at the front is a coaching-sign, dated 1763, giving the distances to London, Worcester, Ludlow, Bristol and Bath. A coach-service to Birkenhead started from the Pied Bull in 1784.

It is said to have been the *old-fashioned inn in Northgate Street* where George Borrow, author of *Wild Wales,* stayed with his wife and daughter in 1854. Borrow seems to have been a man of loose morals, because he was more impressed by the *strapping chambermaid* at the inn than by the quality of the ale and the Cheshire cheese he was served.

*Pied Bull*

*Photo: Mike Penney*

Anyway, people working in the pub have said that they feel an icy presence, beneath the old staircase, in the pub's dark cellar. It may be just a cold draft from a grating, but not too long ago, a respected local historian delved into the Pied Bull's history. What he discovered was quite revealing! This is what he found in the Chester Coroners' Reports for *the second year of the reign of their Majestys William and Mary*:

*'Upon Monday 27th September [1690], the said John Davies did casually fall down a pair of stairs leading to the Sellar belonging to the Pide Bull Inn and with a knife in his hand and thereof languished till this day and about two of the o'clock this morning dyed'.*

People experiencing the death chill had no knowledge, as far as we know, of the sad end of poor John Davies. So what do you think: is there really a ghost or is it just a cold draft?

Why not visit the Pied Bull and check it out for yourself, you're bound to find some sort of spirit!

**The Blue Bell on 'Lorimer's Row' in Northgate Street**
Photo: Mike Penney

# The Old Blue Bell Inn, Northgate Street

The former Blue Bell Inn was part of a small group of buildings known as *Lorimer's Row.*

Its upper floors are built over the pavement to form an arcade. The Blue Bell is, in fact, a fairly intact pair of medieval buildings, extended and made into a single property in the eighteenth-century. The white rendering of the low building conceals the timbering of two-gables, thought to date from the late 14th or early 15th century. The upper storey, over the pavement, has a braced king-post roof. An unusual feature is the detached shopfront between the pavement and the road. At one time the inn had a sign hanging outside in the form of a heavy bell, but it was removed for safety reasons.

The first record of *'the Bell'* is in 1399. The building is very lucky to have survived to the present day. It closed as an inn in 1930, and was to be demolished. After the Second World War it seemed likely that it would have to make way for the inner ring road, which was originally planned to run inside the north wall. However, thankfully, it also survived that threat. For years it was a children's clothes shop, called *Snow Whites*, and it is now a restaurant.

So, the Blue Bell is one of the oldest buildings in Chester. It is not surprising then that it is reputed to have at least two ghosts:

*The young woman whose spirit is still frequently seen is a sad and lonely figure. She is seen looking through the front upstairs window, searching the street below for her lover who never returned. The story goes that during the Civil War the lady waved farewell, from the Blue Bell window, to her Cavalier lover on his way to the battle of Rowton Moor in September 1645. The Cavalier army was defeated, and over 2,000 of the King's party were either killed or captured, and the lady's lover, it is said, was fatally wounded. She never got over her loss and continued to wait, at the window, for her lover, until she starved to death.*

In February 1646, Royalist Chester surrendered to the Roundheads, and they entered the city after a long siege. Roundhead assurances were given that the citizens of Chester and others residents in the city would be:

*Raised and secured in their persons, and their goods and estates within the city and liberties thereof be preserved and kept from plunder and violence of the soldiers.*

However, one poor serving maid at the Blue Bell was to suffer a terrible fate:

*Roundhead troops were billeted all over Chester, including the Blue Bell Inn. One night the soldiers, at the Blue Bell, got so drunk and wild that they brutally raped a murdered a poor serving girl. Now, her spirit can be heard in mortal fear and dread around the building, particular on the twisted and creaky old staircase.*

## The Old Fire Station, Northgate Street

This tall black-and-white mock Tudor building was built in 1911, and is only a short step from the Blue Bell. The structure was built to accommodate three horse-drawn fire appliances. By the 1960s, the fire station had become obsolete. In 1970, a new one was opened close to the Northgate Arena. The facade of the old Fire Station has been preserved, and the building now houses a restaurant.

Behind the old station, and connected to Northgate Street by a covered entry which runs alongside the Fire Station, is Fireman's Square. These cottages

### The Old Fire Station in Northgate Street

*Photo: Mike Penney*

148

were originally built for the fireman, but have since been modernised. Prior to 1911, Valentines Court occupied the site, one of Chester's slum areas, which then contained fourteen cottages, washhouses, a smithy, a stable, and two warehouses.

Just by Fireman's Cottages is a mosaic, set in the ground, commemorating the site of a hostelry called *The Golden Falcon*. This later became the Northgate Brewery, which closed in 1969.

The firemen used to recall that an ancient fireman, with a whiskery face, was often seen around the station, sometimes sitting on one of the older fire engines. He was always dressed in an old-fashioned fireman's uniform, complete with brass helmet. The older engines had large handbrakes with ratchets to hold them on, and these had been seen to move with the handbrakes let off. The old fireman's ghost was nicknamed Jack:

*One night the fireman manning the control room looked through the control room door's observation panel and said he saw 'it' sitting on the old turntable ladder smiling at him. He was so frightened that he immediately threw the bells on and turned out the watch. When the other firemen reached him they said he was as white as a sheet and two firemen had to finish the watch that night.*

Hauntings were not only confined to the Fire Station, it was also believed that the ghost of a woman haunted the little entry, as this old fireman's tale recalls:

*My own experience was on a night duty in the control room. In the early hours of the morning I heard the sound of a woman's high heels proceeding up the cobbles of the entry outside [the Fire Station]. The footsteps stopped and as I waited for her to come in, they started and went back. This happened three times, and when my relief came on about 2.45 a.m. I told him, and he said it was the wind. I replied, "What wind?" and he agreed there was no wind, so we waited, and sure enough, the sound of footsteps was heard again and we decided to catch whoever it was.*

*So my mate went down through the appliance room to the front of the station and we waited. As the footsteps began again my mate went out through the door at the front and I through the one at the side [thus trapping the person in the entry] with the result that we found ourselves looking at each other from either end of the entry which was completely enclosed on both sides and roofed over.*

*We both returned to the control room to discuss this strange happening and*

149

*as we were talking we again heard the sound of retreating steps. This story is a true fact: whether you can offer any explanation I don't know, but my friend and I certainly cannot.*

## The Golden Falcon, off Northgate Street

One of the Golden Falcon's most famous guests was the great composer, Handel, who visited Chester in 1741, while on his way to Ireland. While he was in Chester, he would

*Smoke a pipe over a dish of coffee in the Exchange Coffee House.*

However, like all inns and taverns in Chester, unpleasant events also occurred at the Golden Falcon:

*John Minshull, the Lord Lieutenant of Ireland, used to travel via Chester on his journeys to and from Ireland. While he was on his way to Ireland in 1711, one of his servants got into an argument, with a waiter from the Golden Falcon, over some money that had not been paid for services. The waiter grabbed the bridle of the servant's horse; at this the servant drew a pistol and shot the poor man stone dead.*

*The killer was arrested and thrown into the Northgate gaol. However, Minshull declared that if the man were convicted, he (Minshull) would get a pardon for him from the King.*

*The Mayor of Chester was having none of this and said I will take care that the King and the Lord Lieutenant shall not have any further trouble about this matter and he had the servant executed within a day (or two) after the conviction.*

# The Spanish Lady

## Kiss of Death

**1918. The Angel of Peace laments, "They won't have anything to do with me, but that detestable Spanish woman can go anywhere."**
First published in 'Politiken', Copenhagen

*Real flu hits with the suddenness and power of an express train, puts you in bed for four days, leaves you feeling terrible for a few days more, then with a lingering sense of depression and unease which can last as long as two months. The best that can be said about it is that it is rarely fatal. Only the elderly (sadly) die in any number, and then not of the disease itself but mostly of secondary infections of the lungs.*

Except, that is, in the 1918-19 flu outbreak, which killed between 50 and 100 million people around the world in just a few months. In comparison, within a four-year period, the battlefields of the First Wold War claimed the lives of 15 million people. Most of the victims, uniquely in the history of flu pandemics, were young and fit. The United States lost 50,000 troops in the First World War, but ten times that number to flu. The 1918-19 epidemic lasted just a few months and reached its lethal peak as the war ended.

The 1918-19 outbreak struck first in Kansas, at Camp Funston on the 4th March 1918, and spread rapidly across the globe carried by US troops. However, it was soon dubbed the Spanish Flu, because it was first brought to the world's attention by two cables from Reuters' Madrid office on the same day in June. The first began:

*A strange form of disease of epidemic character has appeared in Madrid...*

The flu's victims included King Alfonso XIII of Spain.

## Tsunamis

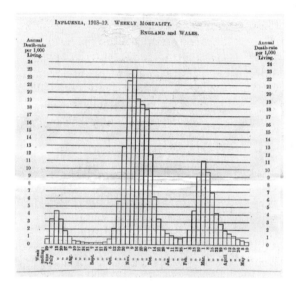

**Three waves of Spanish Flu**

**Mortality figures for England and Wales 1818-19**

Flu epidemics, typically, come in three waves. The first wave of the epidemic in 1918 was severe, but not a killer. It appeared to be the flu that we know today where deaths occurred largely in the very young and the elderly. The second wave hit Brest, on 22 August 1918, and it was lethal. It was nothing like any previous flu and began killing healthy adults between the ages of 25-40. It was often heralded by a violent nosebleed; it attacked the lungs and caused profound skin colouring, as a result of cyanosis (lack of oxygen). It was often difficult to tell if the victim was black or white. Basically, victims drowned in their own fluids:

*There was so much liquid in the air space of their lungs that patents would have bloody fluid coming out of their noses... when they died, it would often drench the bedsheets.*

Coming at the end of the war, it was a huge blow to a world already in agony after the slaughter that Wilfred Owen described as *carnage incomparable and human squander.* The disease criss-crossed the world, killing many more than the Black Death. According to John Oxford, Professor of Virology at St Bart's and the Royal London Hospital:

*You can ask anyone about the bubonic plague, and they will say, "Ah yes, the plague killed a third of Europe." But it still didn't have the impact of the 1918 flu, because bubonic plague killed people over periods of 10, 20, 40, 50 years. Influenza in 1918 killed 50 million souls in a period of one year, and that's why, to my mind, it's the biggest outbreak of infectious disease the world has ever known.*

Five million Indians died, and in Samoa, 25% of the population perished. In the USA, one in 200 of the population died of it, more than were killed during the First World War, the Second World War, the Korean War and the Vietnam War combined. In Philadelphia, corpses were stacked three or four deep in the morgue. By 1919 the virus had reverted back to its old ways, targeting the very young and the elderly. In total, at least 200,000 people died in the UK and, according to the official report, published by HMSO in 1920:

*The mortality in England and Wales...is without precedent in magnitude.*

## *Genesis*

From studies on the 1918 pandemic and on the living flu virus, virologists believe that three factors are likely to increase the risk of creating a monster flu strain. They are lots of people in close contact with live birds and domestic pigs. John Oxford and his team found pathology reports from an army camp in Etaples, northern France, that have given vital clues about the origin of the 1918 pandemic.

Etaples was a huge army camp, almost the size of a city. A hundred thousand soldiers, well and wounded, moved through the camp daily. To supply food to this number, the army installed piggeries at the camp. There is evidence that soldiers bought live geese, chickens and ducks from the local French markets.

Crucially, here were lots of opportunities for the flu virus to move from bird to pig, to soldier. Indeed, in the winter of 1916/1917, Etaples pathologists describe a disease like flu that ended in 'heliotrope cyanosis' and death. John Oxford believes the weight of evidence points toward Etaples as the viral mixing bowl that produced the 1918 strain of flu.

## Lazy Bones

In his *County Palatine of Chester Report of the Medical Officer of Health for the Year 1919,* Meredith Young complained that yet again, as in previous years, many district medical officers (including Chester City's) had not submitted reports for the year, even though he had delayed his report for six months to give them time. This, of course, meant a total absence of information from Chester's medical officer about the flu epidemic in Chester in 1918-19. However, statistics of mortality in Chester are available from *HMS Stationary Office Report of 1920.*

Young did report that 884 people, in a Cheshire population of 600,9180, had died from influenza in 1919. This was about half the number that had died to the disease in the previous year. So that about 2,600 deaths were officially recorded due to flu in 1918-19. There were two outbreaks in 1918 and three outbreaks in 1919. Most of the deaths occurred in the last quarter of 1918, and the epidemic of the first quarter of 1919 was *not so virulent, but some cases proved fatal.*

During the outbreak of flu schools were visited regularly to check on children's health. At the worst time of the outbreak some schools were closed for 14 days, and children were excluded from cinemas.

Hospitals just could not cope with the numbers of flu patients, and Young reported that:

*In some areas it has been found practical to enroll a number of woman possessing a reasonable amount of skill in home-nursing whose services are available  under professional direction  for the nursing of patients during widespread outbreaks of influenza... Provided the right kind of woman is employed, this system is to be commended, particularly when the exigencies of war have produced a large body of educated people who have gained a fair amount of nursing experience...*

One Rural District Health Authority had:

*Fixed a rota of nurses with time at their disposal and passed the St John's or Red Cross classes to help with nursing in times of influenza...*

In addition, in 1919, some District Health Authorities in Cheshire had obtained a supply of an anti-influenza vaccine from the *Government Lymph Establishment.*

# A Chronicle of the Chester Flu Epidemic 1918-19.

Although Meredith Young's report doesn't give details of the epidemic in Chester, all is not lost, because local newspapers do provide valuable information. The following is a diary of the epidemic, with publication dates and headlines as reported by the Chester Chronicle in 1918-19.

<u>26th October 1918</u> <u>*Influenza Precautions  Dr Rennet's Hints for the Public.*</u>

This was the first mention of the epidemic in the Chronicle:

*As influenza is at present epidemic at Chester, the following precautionary instructions, drawn up by the Medical Officer of Health, may be of value*

*... If every person suffering from a fever, with or without symptoms of cold, would stay at home for a few days, the spread of the disease would be greatly*

*reduced...Influenza is very liable to relapse, and pneumonia may occur as late as well as an early complication. Relapse is less likely if the patient goes to bed on the first day of the symptoms, and remains there till the fever has gone...*

*Satisfactory nursing is important in preventing complications and in aiding recovery from a severe attack. The Medical Officer of Health will do what is possible to provide nursing for necessitous cases. The following is useful, both in preventing an attack or preventing complications during an attack... One of the following solutions*

**Prevention is better than cure**

*Courtesy of Cheshire and Chester Archives and Local Studies*

*should be used night and morning as a gargle for the throat and also to wash out the naso pharynx:*

1. *Permanganate of potash-what can be lifted on a threepenny piece. Table salt-level teaspoonful. Water-one pint.*

2. *Boracic acid-teaspoonful, Table salt-level teaspoonful. Warm water-one Pint.*

*The frequenting of badly ventilated and crowded places, such as picture houses and other places of entertainment, is frequently sources of infection, those places should be avoided at present.*

In a final flourish, the medical officer had a dig at Chester's boozers:

*Those suffering from inflammatory conditions of the teeth, throat or nose, are especially prone to catarrhal attacks, Over-fatigue, and, still more, alcoholism, also favours infection. Pneumonia is especially fatal amongst immoderate drinkers....*

2nd November 1819  *Chester's Influenza Epidemic  Numerous Cases and Some Deaths.*

The Chronicle reported that it was estimated that the number of deaths in Chester from influenza and pneumonia since *Last Monday up to this evening (Friday) evening* was about 20 people. It went onto state that:

*The influenza epidemic is still rampant in Chester. There are some hundreds of stricken persons, and some from influenza itself or pneumonia supervening, a number of deaths had occurred. In some cases entire households are down with the epidemic.*

*Doctors are overworking themselves in trying to attend to the numerous calls, and chemists also, in consequence of the phenomenal amount of dispensing, are working at high pressure. Several doctors are themselves on the invalid list, and with the absence of one or two others on military service, the shortage of medical men in Chester is at present being actually felt, and it is hoped assistance may be forthcoming from the National Service Medical Board, whose official duties have been temporarily suspended...*

*Although a general order for the closing of schools has not been issued by the medical officer, several schools are, as a matter of fact, now closed... These closures are due, in some cases to illness of members of the teaching staff, and in others to the spread of influenza among scholars...*

It was announced that the Bishop of Chester had had a slight attack of influenza from which he was recovering, but was *still compelled to minimise his correspondence,* and that Mr. J. T. Hughes, the Deputy organist of Chester Cathedral, was also infected. *Numerous* members of the City of Chester Lodge of Oddfellows and other local friendly societies were also on the *benefit list.*

9th November 1918  *The Influenza at Chester - A Large Death Roll.*

*The returns of the deaths in Chester this week do not afford any hope that the prevalent epidemic has yet exhausted itself. Up to yesterday (Friday) there were 40 deaths from all causes, including 23  from influenza and 11 from pneumonia, as compared with 35 deaths last week, including 14 from influenza and eight from pneumonia... In the months before the epidemic appeared the deaths varied from four to 15, the latter total being registered the last week in August and the first week in July.*

The Bishop of Chester was recovering, but was *still confined to his room.* Mr. A. Stronge, of Crane Street, the Cathedral organist, was not so lucky as the Bishop and died of the flu in the Infirmary. The Chronicle also listed some of the sad details of many victims of the flu; they ranged from all walks of life and age groups. One householder, in Tarvin Road, lost his wife and two daughters, with another daughter and son ill in the Infirmary. There were other cases of multiple bereavements in families.

16th November 1918  *Influenza at Chester.*

This week the Chronicle kept the news of the epidemic short and sweet:

*Since last Friday (Chronicle was issued on a Saturday) there have been 43 deaths in Chester from all causes, including 12 from flu and 14 from pneumonia, compared with 40 deaths last week, including 23 from flu and 11 from pneumonia.*

30th November 1918  *Bovril Advertisement.*

In this edition, the manufactures of Bovril ran the following 'important' advertisement':

157

## Influenza

Bovril Ltd. Wish to express their regret at the shortage of Bovril during the recent Influenza epidemic.

The proprietors of Bovril, recognising that those who are deprived of the bodybuilding powers of Bovril my more easily fall victims to the epidemic, have done their utmost to increase the supply, but the lack of bottles has seriously hampered and still hampers their endeavors. Efforts are being made to collect empty bottles, and it is hoped that supplies will soon be increased by the release of men for the bottle factories.

It is suggested that those consumers who have a stock of Bovril should avoid purchasing at present, and thus leave the available Bovril for those who have more pressing need of it at this critical time.

<u>14th December 1918</u> *Capetown in the Grip of Influenza* <u>Graphic Description of a Dreadful Plague.</u>

It was reported that there were only two deaths from flu in Chester in that week, so the epidemic had probably passed its peak. However, the Chronicle published two letters (dated 6th & 7th October 1918) from a Chester lady, about the flu epidemic in Capetown, South Africa, which the lady found *quaint but surprisingly awkward:*

*Spanish influenza has reached South Africa, and we are having an extraordinary time of it. Natives, Indians and Colonial people generally seem particularly susceptible, and up on the Rand 27,000 natives went down in the first week, and the mines had to be closed. Natives have no fight (immunity), and the deaths have been very bad...*

*V—- (her husband) and I have taken 20 drops of cinnamon each morning as a preventative, and so far, though nearly the whole of the Castle (Hotel) has been stricken down, we have escaped...*

*Our cinnamon has come to an end, and today I have been trying to get some more. V—- tried down in the town, but said it had all been bought up in the shops, which were left open. Then, afterwards, I tried five different chemist shops, but each was closed down with a notice that the whole staff was away ill. Isn't it all quaint, but surprisingly awkward.*

*[Later, both the writer and her husband were seized with the pest, and suffered severely].*

The number of deaths, if any, from influenza or pneumonia in Chester was not published in this weeks issue of the Chronicle. However, over the ages pundits have been only too eager to offer their expert advice on all subjects under the sun, and the paper ran a long article from the Medical Correspondence of the *Times*. His views were, of course, based on contemporary medical knowledge, or lack of it, and he propounded some interesting theories:

*A great deal of nonsense has been written about the nature of the condition (flu)... It is not, however, necessary to assume that any new organism has been present to account for the great virulence of this epidemic. Bacteriologists have long known that the epidemics vary greatly in their severity, and that the passage from host to host may augment the lethal power of a germ until such a degree of deadliness is reached that death occurs within a few hours of infection, and before the ordinary symptoms of the disease...*

The *Times* correspondent also attempted, perhaps rather rashly, to provide a worldwide prospective on the effects of the flu epidemic globally, but with limited information sources, a truly accurate account may never be forthcoming.

*The Flu germ laughs at the doctors*

*Courtesy of Cheshire and Chester Archives and Local Studies*

# The Usual Suspects

There are two types of flu virus, which are of major significance to humans: influenza A and influenza B. Flu is a constantly moving target. The human immune system recognises proteins or antigens on the surface of invading viruses or bacteria as foreign. It then mounts an attack on anything that carries similar antigens. Once infected by a particular virus, the immune system is able to respond to a second attack so rapidly that the disease never takes hold.

Every so often something even more dramatic happens to the flu virus (only to influenza A). The surface antigens undergo a major transformation that makes the virus a complete immunological stranger to the human immune system. Antigen shift, as it is known, is thought to happen when human viral strains incorporate genes from animal viral strains, usually from birds.

There is evidence that the flu virus may find it difficult to hop directly from birds (where it first arose) to humans. However, the domestic pig can be infected by the bird flu strain and by the human flu strain. Virologists believe that pigs might act as a kind of mixing bowl between the bird strain and the human strain leading to an antigenic shift in the virus. Such antigenic shifts are the trigger to flu pandemics.

John Oxford warns of a *time bomb ticking away,* with many world centres having lots of people in close contact with live birds and domestic pigs, just as at Etaples:

*That situation occurs in Hong Kong, but it also occurs in other places in the world, Turkey, Pakistan, Saudi Arabia, South America...We shouldn't really be focussing 100% on Hong Kong, we should be saying, 1918, we know the circumstances, we must look for the same anywhere else in the world which could allow the emergence of the next great pandemic.*

Otherwise, we will need to write another chapter of this book!

# Postscript

Before the publication of this book it was revealed that the deadly SARS virus had broken out under the conditions described above. The disease, it appears, had been hidden by the Chinese authorities. At present there have been no deaths in Chester from the outbreak.